Beholding and Becoming

ORIGINAL ART AND TEXT BY

RUTH CHOU SIMONS

HARVEST HOUSE PUBLISHERS
EUGENE, OREGON

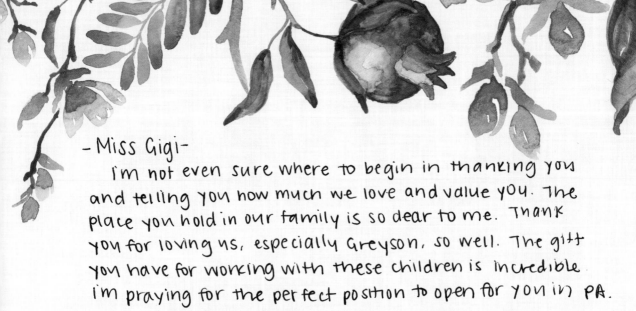

-Miss Gigi-
I'm not even sure where to begin in thanking you and telling you how much we love and value you. The place you hold in our family is so dear to me. Thank you for loving us, especially Greyson, so well. The gift you have for working with these children is incredible. I'm praying for the perfect position to open for you in PA.

Unless otherwise indicated, all Scripture quotations are taken from The ESV® Bible (The Holy Bible, English Standard Version®), copyright © 2001 by Crossway, a publishing ministry of Good News Publishers. Used by permission. All rights reserved.

Verses marked NIV are taken from the Holy Bible, New International Version®, NIV®. Copyright © 1973, 1978, 1984, 2011 by Biblica, Inc.® Used by permission. All rights reserved worldwide.

Verses marked HCSB have been taken from the Holman Christian Standard Bible®, Copyright © 1999, 2000, 2002, 2003, 2009 by Holman Bible Publishers. Used by permission. Holman Christian Standard Bible®, Holman CSB®, and HCSB® are federally registered trademarks of Holman Bible Publishers.

Hand-lettered verses are from various translations.

Cover and interior design by Janelle Coury

Published in association with William K. Jensen Literary Agency, 119 Bampton Court, Eugene, Oregon 97404

Beholding and Becoming

Copyright © 2019 by Ruth Chou Simons (art and text)
Published by Harvest House Publishers
Eugene, Oregon 97408
www.harvesthousepublishers.com

ISBN 978-0-7369-7492-9 (hardcover)

Library of Congress Cataloging-in-Publication Data is on file at the Library of Congress, Washington, DC.

Printed in China

19 20 21 22 23 24 25 26 27 / RDS-JC / 10 9 8 7 6 5 4 3 2

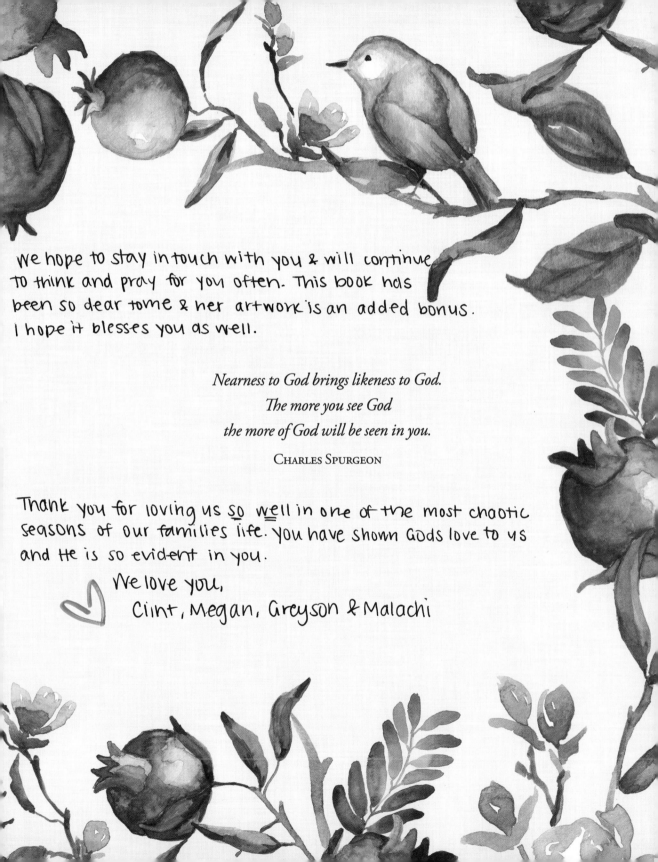

we hope to stay in touch with you & will continue
to think and pray for you often. This book has
been so dear to me & her artwork is an added bonus.
I hope it blesses you as well.

Nearness to God brings likeness to God.
The more you see God
the more of God will be seen in you.

CHARLES SPURGEON

Thank you for loving us <u>so</u> <u>well</u> in one of the most chaotic
seasons of our families life. You have shown Gods love to us
and He is so evident in you.
            We love you,
            Clint, Megan, Greyson & Malachi

CONTENTS

GLOSSARY
A Word About the Paintings in this Book

'm convinced God had the most glorious time forming every detail, design, scent, trait, and oddity in the flora and fauna of His creation. Everything in creation is so intentionally and meticulously crafted to reveal the design of a Master Artist. So, as an image-bearing artist, I think of my job in a very specific way: directing our gaze and awe toward the Creator.

In *Beholding and Becoming*, I've thoughtfully chosen plants, flowers, creatures, and a few other whimsical forms to point to the truth of God's Word and the wonder of *becoming* in Christ. As you take time to savor each page, I invite you to linger long and enjoy the heart behind the imagery.

This glossary expresses my own reflections about what some of the prominent images evoke in me. Use this key to kindle your personal interaction and experience with the text and truths to behold. I painted these for your encouragement…

Bees…workers that produce great dividends

Beetles…unwanted and unfavorable but sometimes secretly helpful

Birds…representative of God's value and care for His children

Blackberries…the thorns and blood of Christ

Bluebells…humility

Butterflies…transformation

Cherry blossoms…fragility of life

Cranes…life, direction

Dandelions…the cares of life

Dragonflies…fleetingness, transience of life

Gingko…perseverance (one of the only trees that survived the
atomic bomb dropped on Hiroshima in World War II)

Honeycomb…fruitfulness and provision

Hummingbirds…continue, remain, and are tirelessly persistent while
discovering sweetness within

Koi…productivity

Lily of the Valley…redemption

Morning Glories…open and close with the start and end of a day

Moths…the temporary, earthiness, fading

Pomegranates…fruitfulness, blessing, abundance

Poppies…remembrance

Thistles…toil and labor

Trumpet Vine…abiding

Sweet Peas…tenacity

Water Lilies…peace

Wheat…harvest and provision

With a nod to English designer William Morris and the Art Nouveau movement of the late 1800s, the paintings throughout this book—like the motifs and
aims of the movement to elevate and revive artistry and craftsmanship in a util-
itarian age—were created to do that very thing as we discover *the art of everyday worship.*

Soli deo gloria.

② Second time through discoveries.

We
Become
What We
Behold

The Art of Everyday Worship

A relatively short time ago, we didn't have an "online life." Tweeting was for birds, posts were for fences, and text required ink. The advent of mobile devices brought a fundamental shift in the way we engage with the world. From the coffee shop to the subway, it isn't hard to find someone head-down with a cell phone. We've been given so much to look at, but we are missing the art of beholding. We are so captivated by our technology and all that it puts before our eyes that we overlook the ways that God displays His glory through creation, relationships, and our ordinary circumstances in the day to day. We look for dramatic ways to experience God, but His presence and transforming work in our lives happen minute by minute.

William Blake may have been the first to say, "We become what we behold," but the apostle Paul certainly defined true beholding and becoming for us who long to become like Christ:

We all, with unveiled face, beholding the glory of the Lord, are being transformed into the same image from one degree of glory to another. For this comes from the Lord who is the Spirit.

2 CORINTHIANS 3:18

The unchanging character of God. Absolutes — Always & Never

We are being transformed into His likeness by looking intently on who He is.

When I was an art student in college, I spent one semester studying the work of Georgia O'Keefe. I was living in New Mexico at the time, where the artist was well known for having painted from a remote ranch in its desert from 1930 to the end of her life. As a budding artist myself, I was enchanted by her body of work, her consistent style, her sense of identity, her fearless expression. She elevated a flower's most overlooked secrets and made grand experiences of its petals and sumptuous lines.

Studying her work wasn't simply acknowledging facts—what brushes she used, what kinds of paint. It wasn't a mere intellectual acknowledgment of her prolific work. No, to behold her art was to gaze upon it with awe, wonder, and willingness to let its beauty change me somehow. Her work impacted the way I perceived nature and even influenced techniques I use in my own creative work.

If admiration and study—even emulation—can cause us to see and respond in an impactful way, how much more so worship—a reverence and adoration for God.

Before you discount yourself as a worshipper, thinking the label too religious, lofty, or spiritual, Paul David Tripp reminds us:

Human beings by their very nature are worshipers. Worship is not something we do; it defines who we are. You cannot divide human beings into those who worship and those who don't. Everybody worships; it's just a matter of what, or whom, we serve.*

---

* Paul David Tripp, *Instruments in the Redeemer's Hands* (P & R Publishing, 2002).

Our jobs, relationships, reputations, and treasures—these are just a few things that compete for our worship. We were made for one worship and one satisfaction, but our taste buds are skewed until our appetites are formed in and for Him.

The question isn't whether we will use our everyday moments to worship because we will—in the midst of ordinary places, people, sights, sounds, joys, and pains. How we direct our eyes, minds, hearts, and hands in the everyday will determine whom we ultimately worship and what we ultimately become. We were made to behold Him and be transformed in Him. The art of everyday worship is the journey from canvas to masterpiece. This is my invitation to you to be transformed, one everyday moment at a time.

1

beholding
God's Greatness in Creation

From the moment we wake, before our feet even touch the ground, we feel the frenzy of the coming day and the pressure to hold it all together and think to ourselves: *I am in control. I am in control. I am in control.*

And sometimes we believe it. We believe we are kings and queens of our own dominions, rulers of our own territories, masters over our reputations and possessions. We are so convinced we're in charge that we ultimately worship our busy lives. Don't believe me? Take a personal inventory: Look at what you spend the most money on, get the most upset about, give the most time to, worry most about, or are most willing to sin to acquire. Take an honest look at what holds these places in your heart, and you'll discover what you worship. Worship is esteeming a thing or a person more highly than everything else and giving it your utmost attention and adoration.

If you're disheartened to find your actions misaligned with what your lips say about worshipping and loving God above all else, consider the possibility that

you need more than a rearranging of schedule and priorities—you need to set your heart on what is truly worthy of worship.

You may remember the account in the Old Testament in which God allowed Job to be tested. Initially Job was unwavering in his faith, proving that his faithfulness to God was not tied to his personal successes and treasures. But in time, the loss, pain, and peer pressure that accompanied an apparent fall of Job's personal "kingdom" exposed a shortsightedness and became an opportunity for beholding God's greatness anew. When doubt crept in, and Job was tempted to take his eyes off God's greatness and instead measure God's goodness against his own, God answered him this way:

> Where were you when I laid the foundation of the earth?
>   Tell me, if you have understanding.
> Who determined its measurements—surely you know!
>   Or who stretched the line upon it?
> On what were its bases sunk,
>   or who laid its cornerstone,
> when the morning stars sang together
>   and all the sons of God shouted for joy?
>
> Job 38:4-7

God called Job to behold a grander view of His greatness through the work of His hands. He painted a picture for Job that, if painted on canvas, would take his breath away—infinite stars, thrashing seas, deepest oceans, tiniest creatures. Belief fuses with trust in the crucible of true worship. And true worship dispels doubt when our grasp of God's greatness in all of creation causes our hearts to surrender in praise. It's impossible to behold what He has made and not be humbled as the created. Beholding God's might causes us to bow low and lift up our praise as Job did:

> I know that you can do all things,
>   and that no purpose of yours can be thwarted.

admiring

"Who is this that hides counsel without knowledge?"
Therefore I have uttered what I did not understand,
    things too wonderful for me, which I did not know.

Job 42:2-3

Perhaps your faith has grown weak. Maybe your aspirations for the growth and security of your personal kingdom have caused you to turn your focus to what *you* can create rather than on the Creator.

If so, it is not too late to redirect your mind and heart as Job did. The full display of God's greatness in creation is right before us if we will simply lift up our eyes and recognize that we are but a "finite creature who has no wisdom to run this world and is utterly ignorant of 99.999% of its processes."* Our loving Father doesn't simply put us in our place to draw out the worship He deserves. He places Himself on the throne of our hearts so that we might see Him for who He is and declare as His creation:

> Let all things their Creator bless
> And worship Him in humbleness,
> O praise Him! Alleluia!

William Henry Draper

---

* John Piper, "Job: The Revelation of God in Suffering," sermon on July 28, 1985.

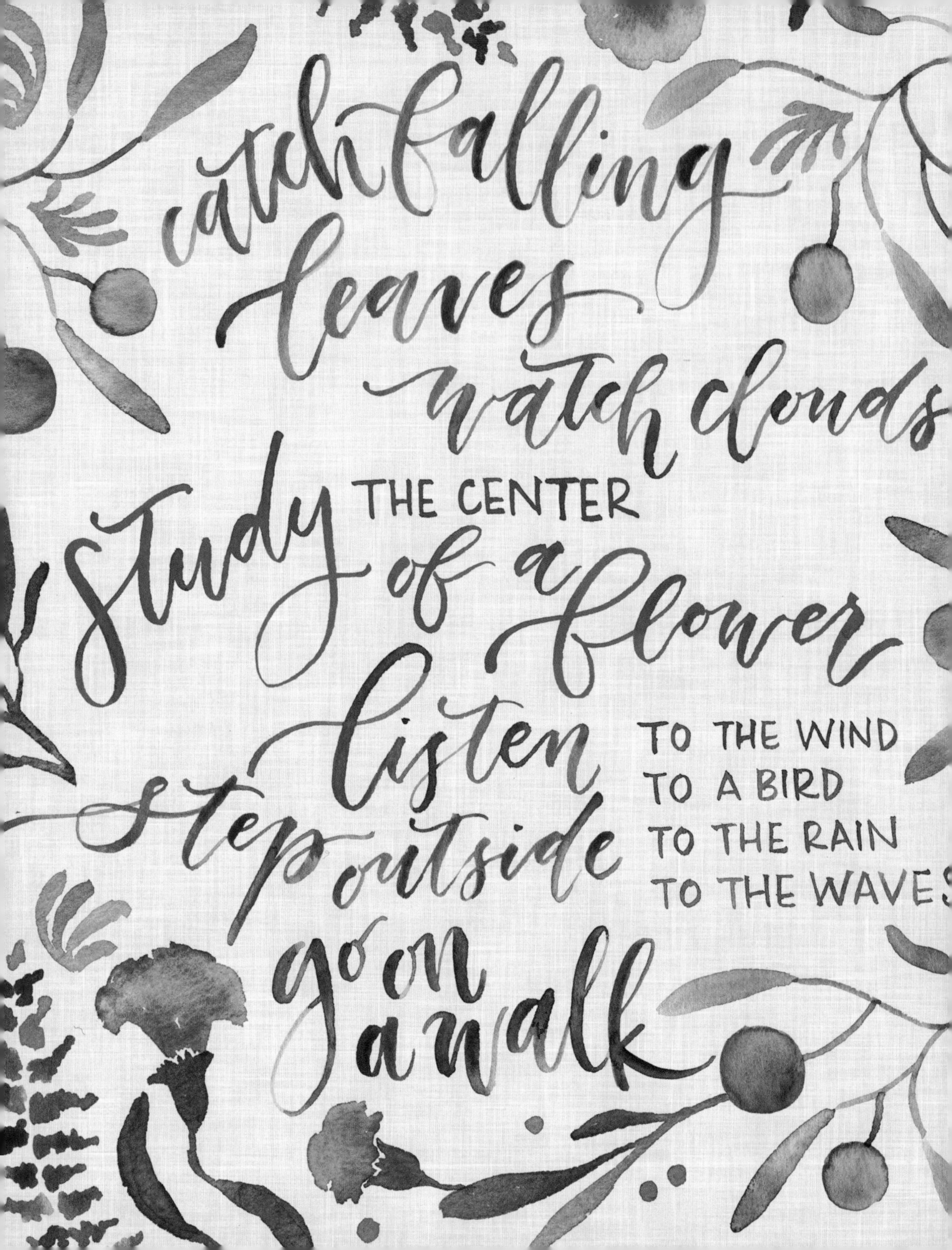

catch falling
leaves
watch clouds
study THE CENTER
of a flower
listen TO THE WIND
TO A BIRD
step outside TO THE RAIN
TO THE WAVES
go on
a walk

becoming

It's Okay to Be Small

God is the Creator; you are the created. God is great; you are not. Does that chafe or relieve you? How you answer that question determines who you are becoming. In our social-media-crazed culture, everyone can be a star. It's so seemingly within reach that smallness feels unacceptable. The entire Internet sends out daily reminders that we are underachievers if we haven't started a nonprofit by age 26, garnered attention from thousands of followers after sharing our talents with the world, or chased fame and fortune. Every generation has wrestled with desiring greatness, but few generations have faced the draw of personal aggrandizement as this one has.

It's impossible for someone to continually behold and be dazzled by personal power and greatness while attributing all greatness and glory to God. The two can't coexist in the same heart. We either become molded by our sense of self-promotion or shaped by our understanding of God's preeminence. Even King David recognized his smallness—not of value, but of power—compared to his great God:

O LORD, what is man that you regard him, or the son of man that you think of him? Man is like a breath; his days are like a passing shadow.

PSALM 144:3-4

Our relative smallness is not a declaration of worth or value, nor does it determine God's attentiveness to our needs. In the very next psalm, David pens the responsiveness of our great God:

The LORD is near to all who call on him,
    to all who call on him in truth.
He fulfills the desire of those who fear him;
    he also hears their cry and saves them.

PSALM 145:18-19

Smallness is a posture of the heart that we take on each day. Rather than stressing out to stake our claim or secure our place of greatness, we know who is already there. Our position of humility in the shadow of His great power is one of relief and freedom because He is near, He fulfills, He hears, He saves. When we behold God's glory in creation, we better understand *His* greatness in and through our smallness.

Worthy are You, our Lord and our God, to receive glory and honor and power;

FOR YOU CREATED ALL THINGS, AND BECAUSE OF YOUR WILL THEY EXISTED, AND WERE CREATED.

Revelation 4:11

2
beholding
God's Faithfulness in a Day

Of all the ways one person can prove his or her love to another, the most tangibly communicated is that of *remaining*: a daughter who remains by her ailing mother's side, a pastor who remains steadfast at the pulpit week after week, a husband who remains faithful to his wife, a mom who remains on the sidelines cheering at a losing game. To remain is to look past the inconveniences, the faults, the unnecessary, and the less-than-ideal, and to say with feet planted and heart unwavering: "I'm not going anywhere." I'd take one faithful friend over a bunch of fickle fanfare any day.

Some of us have felt abandoned, forgotten, or unworthy of being shown faithfulness. "Some of us" is really all of us in the recesses of our private fears and

secret thoughts. We can't imagine a God who will never leave our side in this world of broken promises.

Is it any wonder, then, that the God of the universe chooses to set our days to the rhythm of His unchanging faithfulness—24 hours a day, 365 days a year, year after year? The very measure of a day and its reliability tells us that neither the calling of a day nor its close depends on us. The faithful rising of the sun. Light by which to work with our hands. The warm afternoon sun on our backs. The setting of the sun. The rising of the moon. Stars that never leave their posts. We call these the making of a day, but God calls them a persistent renewing of His faithfulness:

> The steadfast love of the LORD never ceases; his mercies never come to an end; they are new every morning; great is your faithfulness.
>
> LAMENTATIONS 3:23

A day is no random cluster of time. It is ordained and sacred, even when it feels ordinary. If God intentionally directs the rhythms of each day through His creation, not allowing one star to lose its position or one hour to be misplaced, then we are a part of the orchestration of His sovereignty as well, even in the moments we think don't matter.

To behold the steadfast faithfulness of God day by day is to witness His unchanging nature, His relentless orchestration of time and space, and His care over the earth's daily rotation on its axis and each circling of the sun. Each day God displays the reliability of His presence in the most consistent way possible. When we choose to look up from folding the laundry to see the sunset signaling dinner is near, we have opportunity to behold His steady provision of time and consider the work we've completed *good*. He gave those minutes and hours to us. They are not boring, not ordinary, not wasted, but good, simply because He remains.

Then, when the dinner is set on the table and our weary bones shift gears for

The steadfast love of the Lord never ceases; His mercies never come to an end; they are new every morning; great is your faithfulness.

LAMENTATIONS 3:23

DAY by DAY

Worthy of praise

FROM THE RISING OF THE SUN TO ITS SETTING, THE
NAME OF THE LORD IS TO BE PRAISED! PSALM 113:3

all that's left to do before bedtime, the Lord sends out a host of stars and a glowing moon to replace the faithful warmth of the sun. It's a smooth transition to behold. God doesn't miss a beat! He never forgets to send out the moon and stars! He sees you in your ordinary, daily, mundane faithfulness, and reminds you with the steady and consistent rhythms of the day, "I'm not going anywhere." And how that comforts us and causes our hearts to worship!

{ All I have needed Thy
hand hath provided—
great is Thy faithfulness,
Lord, unto me. }

This!

CHASE *sunrises*
AND
be sunsets

mesmerized

BY THE *moon*

COUNT THE STARS
not one goes missing

STOP *toiling*
AND
spinning

becoming

Be Glad in Today

A lifetime is made up of thousands of ordinary moments in thousands of ordinary days. Sure, we have unforgettable dates of significance in our lives: the day we finished grad school, received a prestigious award, led that hostile family member to Christ, welcomed our first child, truly understood the grace of God, or *knew* our spouse was "the one."

And then, some are not-so-ordinary days because they mark unforgettable pain, tension, or sadness: the day we said goodbye to a dear friend, resigned from a job, buried a loved one, learned a difficult previously unknown truth, or finally confronted a wound or wounder.

But most days are lived out putting one foot in front of the other while we "do the next thing," as Elisabeth Elliot famously encouraged through the words of an old English poem:*

> Many a questioning, many a fear,
> Many a doubt, hath its quieting here.

---

* http://www.elisabethelliot.org/newsletters/july-aug-94.pdf

Moment by moment let down from Heaven,
Time, opportunity, guidance are given.
Fear not tomorrows, child of the King,
Trust them with Jesus. *Do the next thing.*

Do it immediately, do it with prayer;
Do it reliantly, casting all care;
Do it with reverence, tracing His hand
Who placed it before thee with earnest command.
Stayed on Omnipotence, safe 'neath His wing,
Leave all resultings, *Do the next thing.*

How we go about doing the next thing has everything to do with what we believe about what we've been given to do and who gives the next breath in which to do it. I think about the verse we know by heart from youth, "This is the day that the LORD has made; let us rejoice and be glad in it" (Psalm 118:24), and I can't help but see the connection anew: When we believe the Giver of every ordinary moment in our every day is the faithful God who is trustworthy for each next step we take in our daily lives, we have reason to rejoice in the gift of another day. "Let us rejoice and be glad in it" isn't a grit-your-teeth-and-obey imperative; it is a response to the preceding truth that this is the day the Lord has made. The Lord is the author of this day you and I get to live. We become joyful and glad about *this day*—today—as we take our eyes off of what we must do and behold the One who created us to do it in the first place.

If God calls this day into existence with us drawing breath by morning, He's faithful to sustain us *in* it. Gladness is the overflow of a heart that recognizes that our cries and victories are not overlooked by a Holy God—neither is our groaning in the toils of every day. Our Holy God is already there, going before us in the steps He's planned for us. This day is holy because He makes nothing without purpose and plan—in this we can truly rejoice.

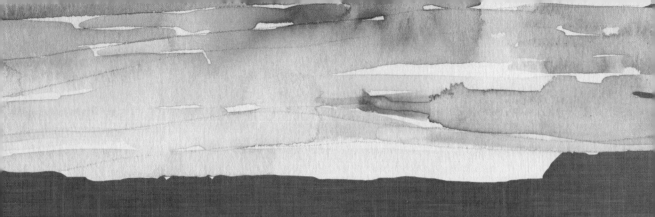

Fear not tomorrow,
CHILD OF THE KING,
Trust them with Jesus
DO THE NEXT THING.

—unknown

3
beholding
God's Provision in the Unremarkable

espite what social media or newsstand magazines try to convey through picture-perfect lifestyle images, no one is exempt from the ordinary aspects of life. Everyone washes dishes, everyone has hard conversations with family members, every person you meet has had to say goodbye to someone dear, everyone does laundry, everyone gets weeds in their yards, everyone collects receipts and documents for taxes, and everyone eventually scrubs out a nasty refrigerator with those spills in the very, very back (you know the kind I'm talking about—why is it always dripping syrup, sticky unknown substances, or raw chicken juice?) where you have no choice but to pull out every last thing only to find you've been successfully providing residence to three half-used bottles of mustard and multiple jars of spaghetti sauce.

If I'm honest, it's not cleaning the refrigerator, washing the dishes, or doing the laundry I dislike; it's the feeling of never being done in the work of the everyday that chafes my checklist-loving heart. No finish line, no fanfare, no award

ceremony. Faithfulness in the unremarkable daily tasks often goes unnoticed—but not to the God who numbers your days. To our all-seeing God, everyday faithfulness is an act of worship and not just an act of survival.

The apostle Paul gave this encouragement to the Colossians, who undoubtedly questioned the value of faithfully serving and working when they didn't receive credit or praise and when the work was tedious or repetitive:

> Bondservants, obey in everything those who are your earthly masters, not by way of eye-service, as people-pleasers, but with sincerity of heart, fearing the Lord. Whatever you do, work heartily, as for the Lord and not for men, knowing that from the Lord you will receive the inheritance as your reward. You are serving the Lord Christ.
>
> COLOSSIANS 3:22-24

Paul was challenging the Colossians not to find motivation for diligence in approval or acknowledgment from others but to find it from continually beholding, in their hearts, their true Master and the eternal treasure waiting for them as children of God. Paul could have encouraged the believers to replace their ordinary labors with more spiritual work, more significant acts of service, or better positions of influence, but he didn't. He simply encouraged them to be faithful—right where they were—in the work before them, powered by the desire to serve God alone.

Friends, what we choose to behold in the midst of tedious tasks and unrelenting responsibilities in the day to day, and what we believe about the God who puts us there, determines whether we see the daily reappearance of dirty dishes and unwashed clothes as a purposeful provision or a nuisance. When we look to the God who provides the blessings and the work that accompanies them, today's tasks become opportunities to praise, to give thanks, and to remember the One we aim to please.

"And whatever you do, in word or deed," Paul says, "do everything in the name of the Lord Jesus, giving thanks to God the Father through him" (Colossians 3:17).

Paige's first verse from West Seattle Christian Pre-K.

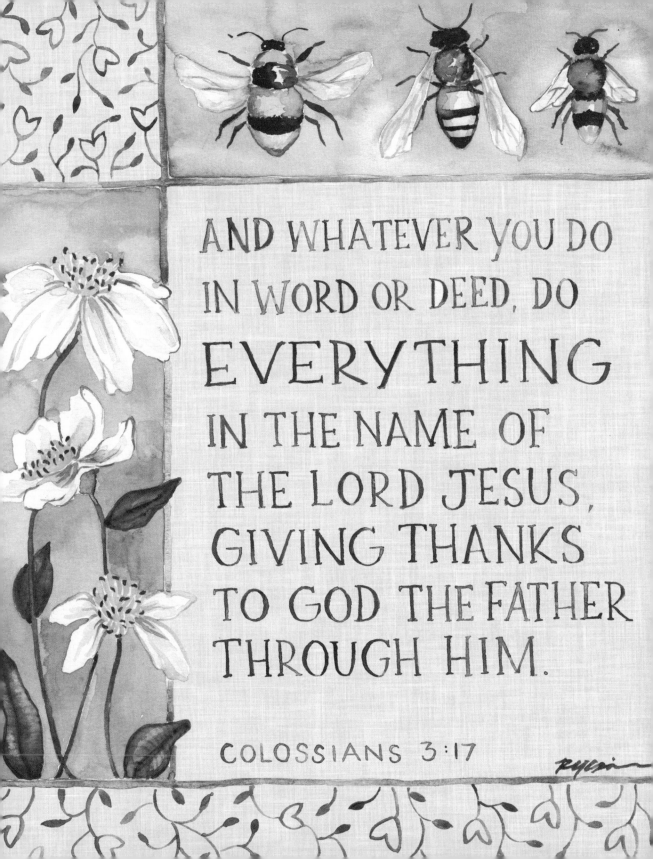

AND WHATEVER YOU DO
IN WORD OR DEED, DO
EVERYTHING
IN THE NAME OF
THE LORD JESUS,
GIVING THANKS
TO GOD THE FATHER
THROUGH HIM.

COLOSSIANS 3:17

listen to worshipful
music or a sermon
WHILE YOU WORK

do something MUNDANE
today to god's glory

celebrate progress

becoming

Learn to Love What Must Be Done

The eighteenth-century German poet, Johann Wolfgang von Goethe, penned these words, which I painted as a reminder to preside over my daily chores:

> Cease endlessly striving to do what you want to do and learn to love what must be done.

In other words, we must stop constantly trying to gain the circumstances we'd rather have, the things we'd rather be doing, the success we'd rather be achieving, the challenges that would be easier to traverse, the praise we'd rather receive. We strive so hard to do what we naturally desire and are so unhappy until we get it. Notice how Goethe didn't say "learn to grit our teeth and do what must be done," but rather "learn to *love* what must be done."

Goethe was not a Christ-follower, but he understood this principle: It's our *love* that drives our joy and regulates how we move through life. That's why Jesus always gave people a new perspective when He gave them a new purpose.

I could try to persuade you to pull yourself up by your bootstraps and love your life. But you and I both know that just muscling through in itself is unsustainable and will never produce joy. It's how and what we love most that shapes our joy. Peter says it this way in his letter to believers facing suffering and unwelcome circumstances:

> Though you have not seen him, you love him. Though you do not now see him, you believe in him and rejoice with joy that is inexpressible and filled with glory, obtaining the outcome of your faith, the salvation of your souls.
>
> 1 PETER 1:8-9

What would cause joy inexpressible in the midst of difficult conditions faced by believers in exile? It's love for Christ, fueled by remembering all that He has done for them, that leaves them rejoicing. We too can rejoice because the transforming power of redemption makes us love what we ought and not only what comes naturally.

Jesus woos us by His love and causes us to love Him in return. If I trace every complaint about my circumstances back to its origin, I find that my addiction to productivity, efficiency, and comfort are always at the center of my unhappiness. At the root of my discontentment is what I love most...and without my loves being reordered and remade by Christ, I will always chase endlessly after what was never meant to satisfy.

It's natural to love what we can see, feel, and tangibly benefit from. That's *easy.* It's supernatural to be transformed and changed in heart so that we are able to love God though we have not seen Him...to trust Jesus though we've never touched Him.

When God spoke to Israel through the prophet Ezekiel, he described the heart change that only God can do:

> I will sprinkle clean water on you, and you shall be clean from all your uncleannesses, and from all your idols I will cleanse you. And I will give you a new heart, and a new spirit I will put within you. And I will remove the heart of stone from your flesh and give you a heart of flesh. And I will put my Spirit within you, and cause you to walk in my statutes and be careful to obey my rules.
>
> EZEKIEL 36:25-27

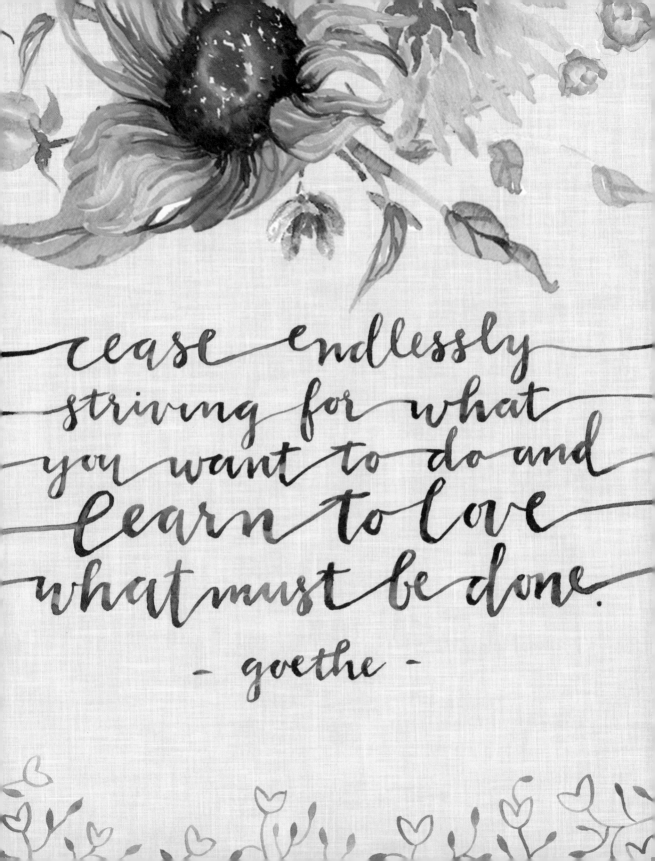

cease endlessly
striving for what
you want to do and
learn to love
what must be done.

- goethe -

do it all
to the glory
of God.

1 CORINTHIANS 10:31

When we turn to Jesus for the forgiveness of our sin and trust Him for the new life we live to His glory, He breaks the bond of idolatry of comfort, ease, pride, and unrealistic expectations. He gives us a new mind and will through a softened heart that desires to please Him. What God revealed here to the Israelites long before the birth of Christ ultimately found its fulfillment in the sacrificial death of Jesus, who enables us through the Spirit to walk with Him, obey, and learn to love what must be done.

We're not duped into loving dutifully; no, the life hidden in Christ gives us a new heart, transplanted through faith in Jesus, which, enabled by the Holy Spirit and powered by the Father's love, causes us to love Him back.

So learning to love what must be done—what is assigned for you to do, what circumstances you have to traverse—is not a form of self-help, attitude adjustment, or esteem building. Rather, it's choosing to do what Peter saw believers doing—preach to ourselves the truth of how we've been rescued and then respond with rejoicing in the here and now.

If faith in Christ means that we are new creations *in Him*, is it any wonder...

...that we begin to love what He loves?

...that what He calls valuable, we learn to find worthy?

...that when the Scriptures tell us that we can do *all things* to the glory of God, including the things we don't desire to do, the things not according to plan, the harder-than-we-can-stand things, the unwelcome pain...that when they tell us "whether you eat or drink, or whatever you do, do all to the glory of God" (1 Corinthians 10:31), we can and are empowered in Christ to do just that?

- *The weary* can *become persevering.*
- *The impatient* can *wait with hope.*
- *The numb* can *become compassionate.*
- *The bitter* can *forgive.*

Those who live a story they weren't expecting—in the mundane or in pain—can "rejoice with joy that is inexpressible and filled with glory, obtaining the outcome of your faith" as Peter says, and learn to love what must be done.

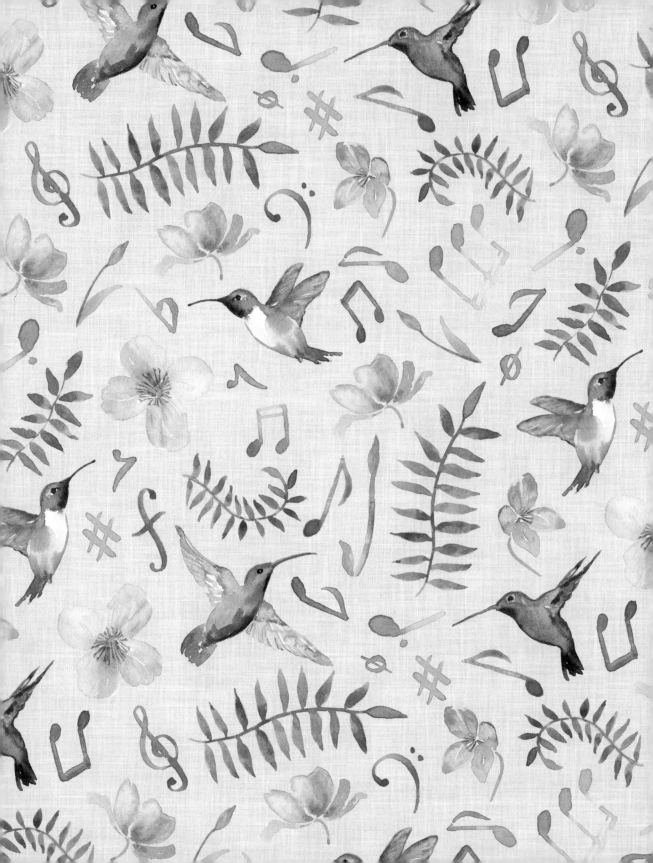

4

beholding

God's Perfecting Work
Through Daily Practice

t seemed like a brilliant idea to have all our boys learn piano...until all of them started taking lessons *at the same time.*

Perhaps you know what it sounds like when someone is learning a piece of music or an instrument for the first time. It's a cacophony of stumbling and fumbling of discordant notes that sound *off.* Most of the time the budding musicians have little to show for their work at the end of a practice—no triumphant trills, no heart-melting delivery of convincing melodies, no exuberant applause for the series of notes hard won after an hour of fingers finding their placement. A day of practice doesn't result in a completed concerto. It's a lot of work that seems to go nowhere, a finish line that you can't see (or hear)...at least *not yet.* As mom to the often-weary boy who's sitting on the piano bench again, day after day, practicing though he can't yet hear the full melody, I've been known to say: *"Child, I know what you don't know. You're going to be thankful for this one day."*

And for us who are weary and unsure if our efforts are headed anywhere, our heavenly Father says the same to us.

Sometimes we wonder how in the world there is not more to show for all our effort.

- *I've been picking up toys all day long, and they're still all over the house.*

- *I've walked every day this past month and still don't see the weight dropping off.*

- *I read my Bible but still don't feel like I get it.*

- *I pick the weeds in my garden, but they always come back up.*

- *I keep repeating the same things to my kids every day—when will they learn?*

Daily practice can feel like drudgery in a results-driven world. How do we stay the course when the road is long and progress is slow?

The writer of Hebrews aptly describes the difficulty in running the race of life:

> Since we are surrounded by such a great cloud of witnesses, let us throw off everything that hinders and the sin that so easily entangles. And let us run with perseverance the race marked out for us, fixing our eyes on Jesus, the pioneer and perfecter of faith. For the joy set before him he endured the cross, scorning its shame, and sat down at the right hand of the throne of God. Consider him who endured such opposition from sinners, so that you will not grow weary and lose heart.
>
> HEBREWS 12:1-3 NIV

We wouldn't be told to throw off hindrances if the course was easy to stay on day after day. The writer of Hebrews paints a picture of a marathon, not a sprint—a race of endurance, not a flashy, one-time display of charisma or

Therefore, since we are surrounded by so great a cloud of witnesses let us also lay aside every weight, and sin which clings so closely, and let us run with endurance the race that is set before us, looking to Jesus, the founder and perfecter of our faith.

HEBREWS 12:1-2

imitating

prowess. God is more interested in how we keep running than how fast or flawlessly we get to our destination.

He calls perseverance the outcome of a faith in progress and tells us how to keep on keeping on with diligence and hope, even when we don't see or feel progress in the now. We're told to fix our eyes on Him. Not on the race, not on the running shoes, not on who is running to our left or right. *Just Him.*

Beholding how Christ endured the cross helps us set our gaze on His provision and not our performance along the course. We don't run in fear but with hope because Jesus is not anxiously wringing His hands but is sitting assuredly next to His Father in heaven. A heart focused on the faithfulness of Christ cannot lose heart in *following* His example.

So take heart, friend: Practice makes *progress*, not *perfect.* The race you're running day by day, the one foot you place in front of the other, the daily choice to persevere, and the diligence to throw off entangling sin—in these God is at work to perfect your faith through your practicing, again and again, the race marked out for you. And with the love of a knowing Father who's gone before you, He assures: *"Child, I know what you don't know. You're going to be thankful for this one day."*

try that thing
that feels
too hard

becoming

Hard Can Be Holy

ur instant culture struggles to embrace the one-day-at-a-time, enduring work of faith. We can't stand for things to be hard. We're so sure there's always a shortcut.

If all the formulas, fads, fixes, and filters that promise to ease the work, speed the process, or boost the ordinary are stripped away, what's left is the doing of the hard things. This reality isn't unpopular just because it's hard (it's actually quite trendy to "do hard things" as they say) but because it requires self-control, perhaps the least heartwarming fruit of the Spirit.

The narrow road of becoming Christlike in your daily walk is the call to do the hard things with self-control: dying to what comes naturally—pride, sin, self-centeredness, appearing strong at all costs, relying on flesh more than on spirit, trusting in yourself—and training yourself to submit to God, body and soul.

The apostle Paul calls it a discipline—an active pursuit—which affirms that our natural bent is to not choose discipline and self-control but to do what comes easily, comfortably, and according to our own desires (I can personally attest to that). He says:

I discipline my body and keep it under control, lest after preaching to others I myself should be disqualified.

1 Corinthians 9:27

Paul equates self-control with safeguarding, and I'm always keen to be hemmed in and protected. Safeguarding from what? From derailment. From sin's disqualifying consequences and deception. Sin promises ease and gratification but hinders, destroys, and takes us off course.

Self-control in itself is not our protection, but walking in the Spirit, which produces the fruit of self-control, *is*. The hard thing you and I are called to do today is not the jobs we do, the places we go, or the people we must love; it is first and foremost the hard work of turning our affections from self to Savior. What at first feels so hard and against our nature becomes welcomed and desired. The running *to* Christ keeps us running *from* sin, and there's no sweeter path than one that's headed where your heart already is.

Till sin be bitter, Christ will not be sweet.

Thomas Watson

To choose obedience and self-control through the power of Christ at work in our lives is holy but hard work. It's holy work to do the hard things you've been given and live according to the new ways you've been called to.

TILL SIN BE
BITTER, CHRIST
WILL NOT BE
sweet.

THOMAS WATSON

5

beholding

God's Example for Family

ind me a woman headed to a family gathering, and I'll show you a sister who's conflicted—both eager to know and be known, and paralyzed in the midst of messy relationships that shouldn't affect her as much as they do. Or show me a mom beginning a new day with littles demanding attention from the moment she awakes, and I'll show you that joy and disappointment, hope and desperation can coexist when it comes to family.

Do you sometimes wonder what God had in mind when He placed us in the families we came from or the ones we now daily work to build? Why my family history? Why these genes? Why this child with these issues? Why me in my weakness?

We don't all have to have the same past, present, or future circumstances to wrestle with questions and perspective about God's design for family.

Family is the first relationship we know and the first human relationship formed by God. I think God gave Adam the job of naming the animals so that he might recognize his need and desire for a partner. But family—the relationship between husband and wife—also experienced the consequence of sin first.

Sadly, the first account of brothers included death, hatred, pride, and selfishness (Genesis 4).

It's no wonder we feel ill equipped and sometimes altogether unfit to handle what it takes to do family well. This side of heaven, family ties are bound to the consequences of sin.

But God chose to use even our broken understanding of family to communicate His perfect relationship with us as our good Father. The Bible tells us that in Christ, we receive...

- *a welcome into the family of God.* "So then you are no longer strangers and aliens, but you are fellow citizens with the saints and members of the household of God" (Ephesians 2:19).

- *adoption as sons and daughters.* "He predestined us for adoption to himself as sons through Jesus Christ, according to the purpose of his will" (Ephesians 1:5).

- *an inheritance with Christ.* "If children, then heirs—heirs of God and fellow heirs with Christ, provided we suffer with him in order that we may also be glorified with him" (Romans 8:17).

- *an Abba Father.* "You did not receive the spirit of slavery to fall back into fear, but you have received the Spirit of adoption as sons, by whom we cry, 'Abba! Father!'" (Romans 8:15).

- *an eternal home.* "We know that if the tent that is our earthly home is destroyed, we have a building from God, a house not made with hands, eternal in the heavens" (2 Corinthians 5:1).

- *unity with the Father.* "That they may all be one, just as you, Father, are in me, and I in you, that they also may be in us, so that the world may believe that you have sent me" (John 17:21).

God created family and sin marred it, but redemption through Christ restores us to our heavenly Father, regardless of whether or not we experience earthly family restoration. When we truly behold the perfect unity between God

For you did not receive the spirit of slavery to fall back into fear, but you have received the Spirit of adoption as sons, by whom we cry, "Abba! Father!"

ROMANS 8:15

YOU ARE NO LONGER
STRANGERS AND ALIENS,
BUT YOU ARE FELLOW CITIZENS
WITH THE SAINTS AND MEMBERS
OF THE HOUSEHOLD OF GOD.

EPHESIANS 2:19

the Father, Christ the Son, and the Holy Spirit, we begin to see the significance of our invitation to be *in Christ.*

We know in our heart...parents are meant to protect, love, teach, and provide. We know in our heart...children are nurtured to obey, trust, depend, and honor. And though this picture of family unity is so often broken in our sinfulness, God's example and design are not.

In fallenness, family relationships can feel too messy, children can seem too difficult to parent, our weaknesses can threaten failure, and our histories can seek to disqualify us. But God rewrites our family tree by grafting us into His. The more we look to God's example for family, the more we discover the freeing truth: Family isn't primarily for our enjoyment or personal legacy. Family is the place from which the gospel is modeled and proclaimed. So the pressure's off, friends. We don't have to have Norman Rockwell family dinners or inspiring stories of generational faithfulness. God uses imperfect families to reflect transformation through the saving and sanctifying work of the cross—one Christ-dependent relationship at a time.

make a gratitude list
for each family member

call your mom

adopt someone who is
far from family

go home and love your
family

becoming

The Mission Field Is at Your Kitchen Table

iven a choice, I would rather have the Lord send me to Africa than clean out my pantry. I'd rather dig wells in impoverished lands, seeing progress and visible fruit, than work through math problems again with my child...or so it seems by the way I esteem the value of ministry to others over the oft-unseen ministry within my own home. So often we are quick to say, "Send me, Lord!" as long as He doesn't send us to the hard soil of difficult extended family relationships or obstinate children, or to the unseen work of sowing the truth of God's Word right within the walls of our messy homes.

Recognizing that my home is a mission field—equal to a remote land or culture—changes the way I think about the people right before me and my reasoning about why God has placed me there.

When I became a mom in my early twenties, I marveled that babies didn't come with owner's manuals. As parents, we look for formulas that will ensure success—a method, order, paradigm, or routine that will ease the "training up a child in the way he should go." We wonder why we must repeat the same things

over and over, why the process feels so unrewarding at times, and whether or not we're even making a difference.

God went to great lengths to instruct His children about instructing *their* children. He helped the Israelites make the connection we need as well:

> Hear, O Israel: The LORD our God, the LORD is one. You shall love the LORD your God with all your heart and with all your soul and with all your might. And these words that I command you today shall be on your heart. You shall teach them diligently to your children, and shall talk of them when you sit in your house, and when you walk by the way, and when you lie down, and when you rise. You shall bind them as a sign on your hand, and they shall be as frontlets between your eyes. You shall write them on the doorposts of your house and on your gates.
>
> DEUTERONOMY 6:4-9

What we choose to repeat at home, practice within our families, and speak about daily directly affects our knowledge of the presence of God and our ability to recall God's faithful works. God's greatness and great story of redemption doesn't just appear within our families by default. It is made known in and through us by deliberate praise and practice.

> And when the LORD your God brings you into the land that he swore to your fathers, to Abraham, to Isaac, and to Jacob, to give you—with great and good cities that you did not build, and houses full of all good things that you did not fill, and cisterns that you did not dig, and vineyards and olive trees that you did not plant—and when you eat and are full, then take care lest you forget the LORD, who brought you out of the land of Egypt, out of the house of slavery.
>
> DEUTERONOMY 6:10-12

God instructed His people to persevere in their work at home while keeping

turning

TURN

YOUR EYES UPON
JESUS, LOOK FULL
IN HIS WONDERFUL FACE
*and the things of
earth will grow
strangely dim in the*
LIGHT OF HIS
*glory and
grace.*

their eyes on their future home. They were to recount and rehearse the faithfulness of God *presently* in every way possible with those in their care so that they and their children would remember to give God the glory when He brought their journey to completion.

When we point to Jesus continually with our praise and practice, we make it known that it is God (and not us) who saves and rescues us from our heaviest burdens.

Mother Teresa famously said, "If you want to change the world, go home and love your family." Sometimes I think we forget that one of the most loving things we can do as parents is to love our children with the full truth of the gospel—not a watered-down story, a feel-good pep talk, or a behavior-manipulating gospel of self-help. That's not the good news. Jesus loved and saved us while we were His enemies, paid the price to pluck us out of slavery, and made us welcome in His presence—*this* is the gospel.

When we speak of this amazing grace in the ordinary routines of our days, we take the good news of the gospel with us to car lines, dinner prep, laundry, and even errands during rush hour—which may as well be the ends of the earth. You see, we are missionaries to our people, right where we are...from the first moments of the day at our kitchen table to the moment we turn down the lights at night.

And when you're weary, mama? Lacking energy, wisdom, or consistency? God calls you to take your eyes off of would-be formulas and fixes or day-by-day desert wanderings in the journey of missional motherhood and turn your eyes upon Jesus in the middle of your days. Friend, keep rehearsing the truth of who He is and what He's done so that not a moment goes by in your family's everyday life without the reminder that God is good and God is near. And as the hymn writer pens for all of us who get distracted at times when we can't yet see the harvest, "Look full in His wonderful face, and the things of earth will grow strangely dim in the light of His glory and grace."

6

beholding
God's Transformation
in Rebuilding

recently discovered a product I hadn't noticed before in the kitchen section of the home improvement store. It was a paint kit that would make a laminated countertop look like granite. I was intrigued. No need to remove the old counter or spend thousands on a new countertop. And no need to wait. If I purchased the kit and started today, I would have a kitchen counter that looked just like granite in no time.

Home improvement stores are filled with folks trying to make what they have a little better. We are experts at patching up, painting over, smoothing out, and hiding flaws. Every time we turn around, it seems, we're having to reseal the deck, repair sprinkler lines, or patch the drywall. If it feels as though everything around you is constantly changing, breaking down, and falling apart...it's because it is. Entropy is at work, and all things are winding down and wearing out. But we've practically made it a national pastime to protect and improve on what we have. Don't get me wrong—I moved into a fixer-upper and love a good DIY home reno as much the next shiplap-loving girl, but sometimes our obsession with improvement blinds us to our need for an all-out rebuild.

That granite-looking counter might look fine—but it wouldn't be granite. It wouldn't be heat resistant or durable like stone. The painted countertop, though looking convincingly like granite from a distance, probably wouldn't add value to the home because the change would be only on the surface.

I think that's why the Pharisees had such a hard time accepting Jesus' teachings. They were eager to preserve, protect, and patch up to look new and shiny—holy on account of the robes they wore and the rules they followed. They tried to find salvation by improving on their own righteousness with a man-made kit filled with formulas, regulations, and a lot of parading around. They appeared to be the real deal, but their holiness was only on the surface.

Jesus taught a parable to show them why He didn't come to simply add on to or repackage legalism and religious formulas. He came to abolish the uselessness of self-improvement and clothe us with His righteousness instead:

> No one sews a patch of unshrunk cloth on an old garment, for the patch will pull away from the garment, making the tear worse. Neither do people pour new wine into old wineskins. If they do, the skins will burst; the wine will run out and the wineskins will be ruined. No, they pour new wine into new wineskins, and both are preserved.
>
> MATTHEW 9:16-17 NIV

Wineskins were the means of carrying wine in ancient times. Old wineskins were stretched out and used to capacity; patching them up to hold new wine was catastrophic. The same is true today for adding a little gospel polish to our sullied, sinful lives; Christ makes us *new*, not better.

Just like a faux-granite painted countertop reveals its real substance when scratched, a spiritual makeover that is surfacy and "white-washed" (Matthew 23:27) will reveal its weaknesses when trials penetrate its glossy exterior.

Jesus offers no shortcuts or cover-ups. He doesn't suggest temporary fixes or cheap alternatives to true freedom in Christ. There's only one way: surrendering the old and gratefully receiving the new. Jesus offers total replacement, and He covers the cost.

refining

restore and refinish
something discarded

throw out and
let go of things
you've
outgrown

fix something
without complaint,
but with thanks

becoming

Seek Treasure That Won't Rust or Fade

f our belongings, homes, comforts, or things are our treasure, we will prioritize protecting and ensuring our well-being and our assets. (No, I'm not talking about the merits of insurance—it's wise to steward what we've been given within reason!) I'm thinking about how often our hearts are wrapped up in the safety and preservation of our material belongings—our homes, our vehicles, our properties, our technology. We fret and worry when our things break down, fearful that we can't maintain the quality of life we've grown to need...or, really, want. We complain and moan when we can't get our hands on the latest comforts, believing that newer and better will get us where we want to go. We talk about our possessions working for us, but if we're honest, it's easy to spend our days working for *them*.

Listen to this familiar Scripture passage:

> Do not lay up for yourselves treasures on earth, where moth and rust destroy and where thieves break in and steal, but lay up for yourselves treasures in heaven, where neither moth nor rust

destroys and where thieves do not break in and steal. For where your treasure is, there your heart will be also.

MATTHEW 6:19-21

What will cause us to want the treasure of heaven more than the treasure of earth? It depends on whether we want temporary or lasting joy. Treasure on earth is valuable...*on earth,* but it loses its worth when our time here has passed. Eternal treasure is invaluable because it dwells *with God,* and we are invited to commune *with Him* forever. Treasure stored up in heaven will never rust, fade, falter, or need fixing because God will never change. To store up treasure with Him is to invest all that you have in what God treasures: the redemption of souls to bring glory to Himself and good to His children.

When we make deposits into the unfading storehouses of heaven, we are building dividends that God multiplies by His faithfulness. Treasure on earth may increase with our nervous self-promotion, guarding or hoarding, and endless hustle, but treasure in heaven multiplies according to our riches in Christ Jesus, which is apparently more than enough for our every need:

My God will supply every need of yours according to his riches in glory in Christ Jesus.

PHILIPPIANS 4:19

So, perhaps more than we realize, we are treasure seekers each and every day. What we chase shapes our race, so don't simply let your heart be your guide. Align your heart with the treasure of Christ, and He will shape your desires and guide your pursuits. And because all that He offers is unfading and untouched by the decay of this world, you can be sure that His riches are more than enough to supply your deepest longings.

but lay up for yourselves treasures in heaven, where neither moth nor rust destroys and where thieves do not break in and steal. For where your treasure is, there your heart will be also.

MATTHEW 6:20-21

7
beholding
God's Will in Every Circumstance

od's will for our lives often feels like a mystery. It looms before us like an enormous cosmic board game that, if played unwisely, lands us the message, "Go back 3 spaces," or worse, "Do not pass go. Do not collect $200." For those who imagine their lives safely within their own control, this game leaves them paralyzed to make the next move or, at best, angry at the indifference of chance. Those of us who believe, even confidently, that God is at the helm of our life's journeys often still wrestle in the day to day, whispering under our breaths: *Could You just let me know Your will, Lord?*

The daily grind doesn't stop to give us time to figure it all out, as decisions impact and send ripple effects throughout our lives. We are in a perpetual war between God's will for our lives and our own will for our lives (and discerning when the two aren't as different as they first appear).

I'm in my midforties, and sometimes God's will for my life feels like a much weightier concern now than it did in my self-discovery-uncharted-path twenties.

My days are not seemingly endless, and not every dream comes true. My child-bearing years are coming to an end, and soon changes to my body will determine much of what I will or will not experience in the second half of my life. I want to know God's desire for my future—my days, my aspirations, my longings. If His will for my life is but a course that determines marriage, children, vocation, and location, I no longer need to pursue His will since many of those questions have already been answered. But God's will for each of us has less to do with who, where, what, and how...than with *why*. And that why knows no arrival to its destination this side of heaven.

In his first letter to the Thessalonians, Paul unlocks the mystery of God's will for our lives. The church in Thessalonica was afflicted and suffering persecution but standing fast in their faith. Paul was writing to those who knew the gospel and were walking in it. And yet Paul—even while commending them for their love, their steadfastness, and their knowledge—chose to remind them of how they were "to walk and to please God" as, he says, they were already doing (1 Thessalonians 4:1). It's as if he anticipated that sometimes, even when we are walking with the Lord, we can doubt our understanding of the will of God and how to continue in it. He specifically tells the Thessalonians that God's will is for them to be sanctified:

> This is the will of God, your sanctification.
>
> 1 Thessalonians 4:3

Set apart and made holy.
He then tells them that God's will is for them to rejoice:

> Rejoice always, pray without ceasing, give thanks in all circumstances; for this is the will of God in Christ Jesus for you.
>
> 1 Thessalonians 5:16-18

Joyful and grateful in all circumstances.
Why would Paul tell the Thessalonians that these are God's will for them...and for us? Because, for believers aiming to be set apart and made more like Christ,

Give thanks in all circumstances for this is the will of GOD in Christ Jesus for you.

1 Thessalonians 5:18

The heart of man plans his way, but the Lord establishes his steps.

proverbs 16:9

every circumstance becomes an opportunity to rejoice and give thanks, having access to the Father through prayer while waiting to understand their circumstances. If a follower of Jesus pursues such a definition of God's will for her life, all the other decisions will fall into place. In other words, God's will is for us to surrender and trust Him with our lives. Whom we marry, where we live, what job we take, how many children we have—how we pursue our dreams is not insignificant, but it's not nearly as significant as whom we aim to please as those plans are revealed.

When we seek to please and honor Christ...

- *with our minds (by remembering the gospel)*
- *with our bodies (by having nothing to do with immorality)*
- *with our lips (by praising and giving thanks in all circumstances)*
- *with our hearts (by praying continually)*
- *with our countenance (by rejoicing always)*

...we won't depend on perfectly planned steps in order to walk confidently ahead. His will for our immediate and long term remains to walk *with Him*, wherever He leads.

make a decision
(get off the fence)

stop worrying about the
future

let go of
your tight grip

recount all the times
God's plans were
better

becoming
Let Go of Control

hough the record shows undoubtedly that my husband, Troy, is a much better driver than I am—with hardly an accident, parking lot ding or mishap, or fender bender with light posts (sigh, I didn't see the concrete structure the light post sat on), and no ill-timed left-hand turns—I still close my eyes when he's passing other vehicles. It makes no sense, but it's revealing: I like to be in control. Even if my own track record is faulty or untrustworthy, I'm wired to think myself safer with my own hands on the steering wheel.

Isn't that what drives our incessant need to know the future and to manage everything in our lives? We call it planning—purposeful, and proactive—but if we're honest, it's often our belief that we know better than God and could orchestrate circumstances better than Him if we only had access to all variables.

- *I could avoid pain and suffering if I only knew what will happen next.*

- *I could avoid relationship conflicts if I could manage others' perceptions of me.*

93

- *I could avoid frustration if I could just make sure my husband does it my way.*

- *I could avoid failure if I make sure I make the right decisions.*

What we are really saying when we try to control and manipulate the circumstances of our own lives is this: *I can avoid having to trust God if I can simply trust in myself.*

We are naturally bent toward believing ourselves to be all wise, all powerful, all capable. We know our own track record, and yet, we want the reins. If a faulty view of ourselves results in a fatal belief about who is in control, then a right view of God and His sovereignty can shape our hearts to trust Him alone.

> Not to us, O LORD, not to us, but to your name give glory,
>   for the sake of your steadfast love and your faithfulness!
> Why should the nations say,
>   "Where is their God?"
> Our God is in the heavens;
>   he does all that he pleases.
> Their idols are silver and gold,
>   the work of human hands.
> They have mouths, but do not speak;
>   eyes, but do not see.
> They have ears, but do not hear;
>   noses, but do not smell.
> They have hands, but do not feel;
>   feet, but do not walk;
>   and they do not make a sound in their throat.
> Those who make them become like them;
>   so do all who trust in them.

PSALM 115:1-8

St. Patrick's Breastplate

Christ

be with me
within me
behind me
before me
beside me
to comfort
to win me
and restore me
Christ beneath me
above me
in quiet
in danger
in hearts of
all that love me
in mouth of
friend and stranger.

ALL THE WAY MY SAVIOR LEADS ME; WHAT HAVE I TO ASK BESIDE? CAN I DOUBT HIS TENDER MERCY WHO THROUGH LIFE HAS BEEN MY GUIDE?

- FANNY CROSBY -

The psalmist does not mince words: Our God does all that He pleases.

And while we may not consider them idols, our safety nets of control, strategy, manipulation, and wearing ourselves thin trying to keep all perceptions and plans going our way…well, they fail us and show themselves to be hollow forms of security—man-made idols that cannot save or secure. When we serve those, we become *like them*.

Friend, when we are tempted to serve the idols of control and self-assurance, let us remember them for what they are—false and deceiving masters. Let's turn instead to our sovereign and faithful God, who does all that He pleases to bring Himself glory while He demonstrates His steadfast love. When we place our need for control within His hands, we become reflections of His glory and steadfast love. And that, dear friends, pleases Him very much.

This my song through endless ages, Jesus led me all the way.

8

beholding
In Praise of Failure

We avoid it, hide it, and sometimes deny it, but sooner or later, we all fail. Even to write those words feels defeating when we want to believe we're products of our own strength and strategies. To take a spin around social media, a dinner party, or even a play date at the playground is to believe that failure is optional, that we can bypass the pain and frustration of falling short if we simply try harder or plan better. But the truth is that 100 percent of all people are guaranteed to fail regardless of how well they scheme, prepare, execute, or hustle.

What great lengths we go to as we try to outdo, outsmart, be the best, or succeed in big and small ways. Even if we don't aim to be number one, we're afraid of coming in last. I remember a friend asking me years ago, during a fearful season of risk in my life: "What's the worst thing that could happen?" My reply was so simple: "Failure, I guess." But what is, ultimately, so scary about failure? It's

not failing in itself that is frightening. It's the damaged reputation; loss of trust, image, or approval; or an unwanted "I told you so" from naysayers that scares us.

I think we worship our own reputation more than we realize. Our pursuit of success and our skirting of failure are really campaigns for authority and power in our own lives. We grasp for self-centered security and deny dependence and weakness.

A quick tour around the subjects represented in my personal library reveals my own fight against messing up or missing the mark:

- *how to manage excess weight*
- *sleep training*
- *parenting teens*
- *making a lasting marriage*
- *secrets and tools used by successful people*
- *financial planning*
- *battling your anger*
- *how to read the Bible*

But no matter how many books I purchase or strategies I employ, the fact remains that I fail on a daily basis in these areas and more. You see, the temptation for me (and perhaps for you) is to strategize my way to never fail. Being defined by our successes and failures is how this world operates, even if unspoken. But God—He makes no secret of our faults and frailties. In fact, He gave the Law (remember the Ten Commandments?) to show us what His good and perfect standard is...and how incapable we are of meeting those requirements.

Failure and shortcomings remind us that we are not saviors of our own lives. They keep us tethered to the humbling reality that in order to receive the grace of God, we must begin by believing we are in desperate need of it.

Have you messed up within relationships? Do you know the sting of demotion?

Our greatest fear
should not be of
failure, but of
succeeding at
something
that doesn't
really matter.

D.L. MOODY

aligning

Have you known the shame of not doing what you said you'd do? Do you fear and worry about disappointing others? I have and do regularly. If your hope is in Jesus the Savior, these daily failures and inconsistencies do not define you before a holy God but drive you to gratefulness for His saving grace that doesn't leave you there. God allows us to feel the weight of our shortcomings so that we might behold the abundance of His grace.

But the apostle Paul instructs us to consider God's grace rightly: "What shall we say then? Are we to continue in sin that grace may abound? By no means! How can we who died to sin still live in it?" (Romans 6:1-2).

We embrace and welcome failures, not as an invitation or license to sin but as surrender to a holy God, who loves us enough not simply to point out our failures but to free us from the shame of them. Do your weaknesses and failures leave you feeling condemned, or do they lead you to the throne room of God? Do they cause you to grovel or give thanks?

Paul again reminds us what is ours in Christ:

> There is therefore now no condemnation for those who are in Christ Jesus. For the law of the Spirit of life has set you free in Christ Jesus from the law of sin and death. For God has done what the law, weakened by the flesh, could not do. By sending his own Son in the likeness of sinful flesh and for sin, he condemned sin in the flesh, in order that the righteous requirement of the law might be fulfilled in us, who walk not according to the flesh but according to the Spirit.
>
> ROMANS 8:1-4

Friend, if our response to failure is to cover it up and to present ourselves as other than we actually are, we prove ourselves idolaters—of ourselves. The same is true if our response is self-condemnation and self-pity. These are not the responses of beloved children but of contenders for the throne of God in our own lives. But if we respond to failure, big or small, by beholding the price Jesus

paid to make us defined by His accomplishment and not our own, we align our hearts with worship of Him and receive forgiveness as grateful children.

Believer, God isn't making excuses, skirting the issue, or turning a blind eye to your failures. Neither is He crossing His arms in silent disapproval, withholding His care until you get it right. To believe so is to miss the wonder of the gospel entirely. In the everyday mistakes or in the failures of a lifetime, God calls us out of hiding and pays the price for our freedom. We can stop fearing failure. Our regrets, mishaps, and mess-ups are no longer the final word over our lives. Jesus' victory on the cross is.

BE
FAITHFUL
WITH THE
SMALL
THINGS.

admit a shortcomin

give thanks for one thing that
feels like failure

celebrate small successes

be faithful with something small

becoming
Discover True Success

Thanks to ever-current updates broadcast for all to see in our time in human history, we don't have to look far to find someone living their best life, reaching their highest potential, or accomplishing amazing feats, and all with seemingly little strain, cost, or periods of unglamorized, unseen hard work. It's normal in our day to catch everyone's highlight reels and forget how many feet of everyday footage lie on the cutting-room floor.

These often go unseen...

Authors, who've spent countless hours journaling, blogging, scribbling notes on napkins, honing their craft, and reworking their syntax for breakthrough.

Moms, who spend their days with children on their laps, instructing, reinstructing, over and over.

Painters, whose layers upon layers on a canvas tell a journey far beyond what is on the surface.

Athletes, who set their alarm clocks for practice in spite of their comfort or feelings.

Pastors, who pore over the original Greek or Hebrew for weeks, praying through the meaning of the ancient text to bring God's Word to a modern people.

Entrepreneurs, doing what it takes day after day to see a sprout of an idea take root.

Godly men and women, who wrestled doubt, anger, grief, and pain long before their testimonies of unshaken faith and confidence in the Lord are known.

These are not usually the pictures of success we see as we scroll through our devices. Success is defined by achievement, victory, and accolades, and sometimes we're tempted to believe that it looks like one's name in neon or a headline, or a number indicating x number of followers. But Jesus defined success differently.

Jesus came to earth through an ordinary young couple who worked with their hands. He was born in a stable fit for animals, called lowly and simple men to serve with Him, and rode into Jerusalem for His appointment with the cross on the back of a donkey. He gathered the needy, hungry, sick, and poor. His name made the news, but not favorably, among those who mattered in the social arena. His community defined success by regality, and, well, not being crucified as a criminal. But Jesus demonstrated success by doing exactly what the Father gave Him to do. For Jesus, faithfulness was success.

In Matthew 25, Jesus taught about faithfulness through a parable—the Parable of the Talents. In it we read about a master who entrusted three servants with the same number of talents (a unit of value) and the care of his property while he was away:

> Now after a long time the master of those servants came and settled accounts with them. And he who had received the five talents came forward, bringing five talents more, saying, "Master, you delivered to me five talents; here, I have made five talents more." His master said to him, "Well done, good and faithful servant. You have been faithful over a little; I will set you over much. Enter into the joy of your master" (verses 19-21).

FAITHFULNESS
IS SUCCESS

the steps of a man are
established by the Lord,
when he delights in his
way; though he fall, he
shall not be cast headlong,
for the Lord upholds
his hand.

PSALM 37: 23-24

But the parable ends with the third servant coming to his master, having done nothing with what he was given, to his master's displeasure. Jesus taught this parable to simply illustrate that God gives His children gifts for His glory; we are to use them and to be faithful with what we've been entrusted, great or small. The parable does not highlight what personal greatness was achieved; instead, it highlights success as faithful stewardship for God's glory and not our own.

What difference does it make in our day-to-day lives when we steward even seemingly insignificant opportunities with faithfulness? Jesus faithfully did the work of His Father, even to nail-pierced hands. What you do may not look like titles, badges, or letters behind your name, but God's pleasure in your everyday faithfulness will be your name graven on His hands and His welcome when it matters most: *Well done, good and faithful servant. You have been faithful over a little; I will set you over much. Enter into the joy of your master.*

9

beholding

How to Measure Abundance and Plenty

read one time that even the humble carnation looks luxurious en masse. While a single flower is profoundly beautiful in its own intricate design, we were made to be in awe—*to gasp*—at a sea of blooms. Abundance and plenty stir the heart, provoke praise, and fuel deep gratitude. Compared to drought and famine, a field overflowing with harvest is relief, joy, and satisfaction.

It's no wonder, then, that Jesus made His purpose clear: "I came that they may have life and have it abundantly" (John 10:10). But many of us, as God's beloved children, live the daily grind on empty, lacking _____, and feeling "not enough." We operate like beggars in the house of the King. *We were made for more.*

A hidden camera in my house would likely catch me slumped-shouldered, bemoaning how I lack what it takes to accomplish what God has given me to do. It would find me secretly sighing at home repair costs and grocery bills. It would capture my oft half-tank attempts to hustle while my Bible-fuel sits on the shelf.

How is it that we are quick to acknowledge the God of the wilderness—the One who leads us through the desert and takes us through parched seasons—but not so much the God of abundance? Anyone who's wandered a desert season knows the deep satisfaction of entering a land of milk and honey. But like the Israelites, we so easily forget. We trust Him to save us *from* spiritual bankruptcy but forget that He saves us *to* soul abundance. We're not just rescued from death and destitution; Jesus came to give us abundant life. (I'm not talking about material things, though He astoundingly grants us more than enough as well.) *Abundance. Plenty. Fullness. Overflowing.* I'm the first to admit that these words are rare in my vocabulary and seem perhaps contraband in the life of the believer. They shouldn't be.

Our God operates out of plenty, but we don't often behold Him that way. I think that's why the Bible so often reminds us that He is the source of all abundance:

> You prepare a table before me in the presence of my enemies; you anoint my head with oil; my cup overflows—Psalm 23:5.

> And God is able to make all grace abound to you, so that having all sufficiency in all things at all times, you may abound in every good work—2 Corinthians 9:8.

> They feast on the abundance of your house, and you give them drink from the river of your delights—Psalm 36:8.

> And my God will supply every need of yours according to his riches in glory in Christ Jesus—Philippians 4:19.

> Now to him who is able to do far more abundantly than all that we ask or think, according to the power at work within us—Ephesians 3:20.

Do you remember Jesus' encounter with the woman at the well in John 4? He went to meet her at the heat of the day, when she, a disgraced, serially

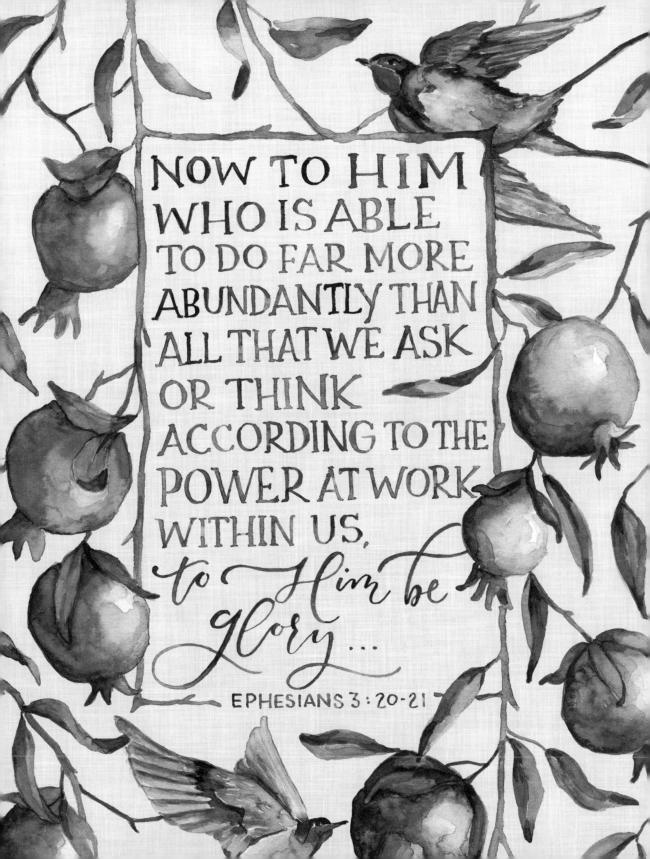

NOW TO HIM
WHO IS ABLE
TO DO FAR MORE
ABUNDANTLY THAN
ALL THAT WE ASK
OR THINK
ACCORDING TO THE
POWER AT WORK
WITHIN US,
to Him be
glory ...

EPHESIANS 3 : 20-21

ascribing

promiscuous Samaritan woman, could draw water without harassment or public shame. Jesus didn't just uncover her self-satisfying sin and expose her lack of understanding ("I can give you living water." *"But you don't have a pail."*); He offered her unending satisfaction through Him. He didn't just show how empty she was; He offered her abundance and fullness: "Everyone who drinks of this water will be thirsty again, but whoever drinks of the water that I will give him will never be thirsty again" (John 4:13-14).

The Samaritan woman couldn't receive all that Jesus offered until she recognized that He was better than her hidden sin. After meeting Jesus, she knew what it was to be truly filled up. She understood that abundance had nothing to do with the pail or vessel, but everything to do with what was inside.

Just like the woman at the well, we must come to the end of our vain pursuit of abundance to receive His. We miss the generous bounty God offers when we are fixated on measuring our own resources. We forget that Jesus saves us to new life by offering His unending, overflowing supply of mercy and grace.

Degrees, bank accounts, followers, accomplishments, possessions...we can blindly measure abundance according to our own means. Or we can behold the great bounty that is ours through faith in Jesus. And just as He did with the Samaritan woman, Jesus replaces our shame with assurance, our endless thirst with true satisfaction, our useless fillers with fullness in Christ. He makes us, who were beggars at the door, children at the King's table—a table that overflows with the richest fare. And when we, the hungry and forgetful, come to it, we find anew that Jesus is the full measure of abundance and life.

count your
blessings

what has He done
that is more
abundant than
you asked for?

name one of
your riches
in Christ

empty
your online
shopping cart

becoming

You're More Than Your Money

For whatever reason, when my husband, Troy, and I got engaged more than 20 years ago, I was, at the time, not interested in registering for newlywed *stuff*. Imagine a man coaxing his fiancée to choose the color of bedding, towels, and dishes she wants their loved ones to purchase for them. It was like pulling teeth (according to him), and that afternoon with the handheld scanner will go down in Simons history as one of the most aggravating experiences of our early romance. So you can imagine his surprise when, a few years later, I became a decor-hunting, platter-loving, table-setting, curtain-sewing hoarder of lots and lots of *stuff*.

Let's be clear: I have no problem loving and wanting things for my home anymore. I'd happily register for new linens, towels, dishes, mixing bowls, candleholders, Dutch ovens, and tea towels if someone handed me a scanner now. I have a constant desire for material things—things that make me feel prettier, more efficient, more equipped, more stylish, more updated...more, more, more. The love of things, at its root, is a love of comfort, appearance, approval, pride,

security, or ease. When the Bible tells us that the love of money is a root of all kinds of evils, we can trace that love back to our love for ourselves, foremost.

> But those who desire to be rich fall into temptation, into a snare, into many senseless and harmful desires that plunge people into ruin and destruction. For the love of money is a root of all kinds of evils. It is through this craving that some have wandered away from the faith and pierced themselves with many pangs.
>
> 1 Timothy 6:9-10

At its core, the love of money is the desire for what money can acquire for us—all that we think we can have to satisfy ourselves apart from abundance in Christ. That craving, the craving to secure our own satisfaction, causes us to wander away from dependence on Jesus. You see, you can't chase self and worldliness *and* run toward Jesus at the same time. We become what we behold. If we set our face toward the love of money, we will have the likeness of earthly desires, more and more.

> The sorrows of those who run after another god shall multiply.
>
> Psalm 16:4

But subtler than a blatant chasing after the god of money are our day-to-day patterns that form a routine, and a routine that sets a course—the way water carves a chasm little by little, year after year. Daily choices make deep channels. Timothy warns about letting our desires wander little by little because we will begin at one point and end up at another without realizing it.

- *Does anyone set out to be deceived by the promises of money?*
- *Does anyone plan to feel unsatisfied, always wanting more?*
- *Does anyone purpose to make an idol of self-indulgent pursuits?*

No, these are destinations we wander to when we don't run to Jesus with our

ABUNDANCE

desire and need. When we don't aim Christward, we will certainly find ourselves wandering into the snare of worldly desire. Our enemy, Satan, is not neutral. He actively works to distract us with seemingly harmless desires that ultimately lead to destruction.

If money is the fuel for the fire of our worldly desires, we can catch on fire without knowing how close we're standing to the flame. To not let money bind and capture our hearts is a matter of deliberate redirection of the heart, day by day, moment by moment.

Jesus cut to the chase when He addressed the heart through a parable:

> He said to them, "Take care, and be on your guard against all covetousness, for one's life does not consist in the abundance of his possessions."
>
> LUKE 12:15

The question today is not about how much stuff we want or have, nor is it about how much is too much. Abundance begins with a heart that stores up its true treasure in Christ. When our treasure is with Him and not with our possessions, we'll guard that treasure and long for more of what is *good*.

10
beholding
Jesus in Our Words

You and I have a superpower we take for granted every day. It's not only for the strong, skilled, gifted, or pedigreed. This superpower doesn't take into account age, rank, or occupation in life. It cuts, exposes, forms, and fashions through everyone who wields it. And often we moan our lack of impact, impotence to make a difference, and powerlessness, never grasping the weight and wonder of this superpower at our disposal each and every day…the ordinary, yet extraordinary, power of words.

But let's start here: The very DNA of existence was called into being by four simple words, "Let there be light," spoken with decisive care by our Creator. God, the maker of heaven and earth, is also the one who described Himself with the first and last letters of the Greek alphabet: "'I am the Alpha and the Omega,' says the Lord God, 'who is and who was and who is to come, the Almighty'" (Revelation 1:8).

The power of words is so vividly woven into the expression of God's design for His children that the apostle John calls Jesus "the Word"—*logos*—the One who spoke and embodied the entire declaration of redeeming love to the world:

> In the beginning was the Word, and the Word was with God, and the Word was God. He was in the beginning with God. All things were made through him.
>
> JOHN 1:1-3

If that sounds familiar, it should. Jesus Himself spelled it out and connected the dots between Himself, the Father, the Word of God, and the message of truth:

> I am the way, and the truth, and the life. No one comes to the Father except through me.
>
> JOHN 14:6

In other words, God cared so much about getting His love letter of hope and salvation into our hands that He was willing to send His Son to be the message—to be the final word on everything God wants us to know about Himself.

As children of God, we are given the good news—not merely strung together as words on a page, but as the living Word embodied in we who are transformed and redeemed.

But so often in my own life, harsh, condemning, and complaining words are present more than faith-filled, life-giving ones. We need the truth: When we use careless, hurtful, or manipulative words, we are marring the very Word we bear—*Christ in us*. Why do such things come from our lips, then?

Our words don't always reflect the message we carry because we don't always believe Jesus *is* the final word. Idle words reveal our idols because the words that come out of us betray what we worship in silence. We either believe that God's Word is true, His plan is good, and His ways are trustworthy, or we believe that we ourselves speak the truest words. The power of words wielded by one who thinks he or she knows better than God will always leave others wounded,

Gracious words are like a honeycomb, sweetness to the soul and health to the body.

PROVERBS 16:24

betrayed, hurt, or cut down. We can't behold Jesus as the truth and go on speaking as if *we* are.

- *When children are disobedient or disappointing, do I communicate words that God is the rescuer and not their good works?*

- *When a spouse discourages, do I respond as one who finds Jesus enough?*

- *When the plan goes awry, do I declare Him faithful or myself a failure?*

- *When others wrong me, do I lash out in fear or speak truth in love?*

Don't feel condemned by your answers, friend; instead, behold the goodness and glory of God anew, and come under God's power to supernaturally transform your words and thoughts as He did with David in Psalm 19:

> The heavens declare the glory of God,
> and the sky above proclaims his handiwork.
> Day to day pours out speech,
> and night to night reveals knowledge.
> There is no speech, nor are there words,
> whose voice is not heard.
> Their voice goes out through all the earth,
> and their words to the end of the world (verses 1-4).

When our gaze turns to worship, and our worship responds to the declarations of our God, we can't help but find this the bent of our hearts:

> Let the words of my mouth and the meditation of my heart
> be acceptable in your sight,
> O LORD, my rock and my redeemer (verse 14).

hold your tongue
choose words of
life

affirm someone

hide God's Word
in your heart

becoming
Speak from Overflow

As hard as we try to keep up with appearances, it's our lips that are most telling about who we really are. We may put on cloaks of nice clothes, nice homes, nice friends, nice jobs...but the things we say at home, at work, and online can show us to be walking around in the emperor's new clothes. If nothing else, comment threads and Twitter feeds serve to prove the depravity of man. Behind the false protection of the screen, many of us throw out self-control, gentleness, humility, teachableness, and the honest good sense of holding our tongue in the online forum. We take dozens of selfies so we can post just the right one but leap before we think when it comes to making our opinions known.

Stress doesn't cause ugly attitudes and behavior; it reveals it.

No wonder James writes so famously about the tongue, and warns those who are unbridled in their speech:

> If we put bits into the mouths of horses so that they obey us, we guide their whole bodies as well. Look at the ships also: though they are so large and are driven by strong winds, they are guided

by a very small rudder wherever the will of the pilot directs. So also the tongue is a small member, yet it boasts of great things.

How great a forest is set ablaze by such a small fire! And the tongue is a fire, a world of unrighteousness. The tongue is set among our members, staining the whole body, setting on fire the entire course of life, and set on fire by hell. For every kind of beast and bird, of reptile and sea creature, can be tamed and has been tamed by mankind, but no human being can tame the tongue. It is a restless evil, full of deadly poison. With it we bless our Lord and Father, and with it we curse people who are made in the likeness of God. From the same mouth come blessing and cursing. My brothers, these things ought not to be so.

JAMES 3:3-10

James makes clear his warning: The tongue is small but powerful. Untamed, it can do much harm.

But the answer isn't politeness. It's not about communication style or being an extrovert or an introvert. No, the taming of the tongue is an issue of the heart:

A good man produces good out of the good storeroom of his heart. An evil man produces evil out of the evil storeroom, for his mouth speaks from the overflow of the heart.

LUKE 6:45 HCSB

In other words, how we use our tongues directly reveals the condition of our hearts. If we think bitter thoughts and believe God has given us the wrong circumstances, our lips will reveal that bitterness. If we judge or hate in our hearts, sooner or later our tongues will betray that sin. If we—at the core—believe God to be less than He is and unworthy of our utter obedience, we will speak as ones who think ourselves rulers of our own kingdoms. You see, we can try to white-knuckle niceties or refrain from ugliness in moral conformity, but if we don't

FOR OUT OF
the overflow of the heart
THE MOUTH SPEAKS
— LUKE 6:45 —

address the heart, our efforts are in vain and will have no lasting effect. Just as the tongue can steer the whole person, so the heart steers the tongue.

The hallmark of a mature Christian is that he or she knows how to speak when it's costly, to remain silent when there's freedom to speak, and to discern what is best for the glory of God. If that convicts you as it does me, let it drive you to evaluate your heart rather than to accept defeat. It is so easy to throw up our hands and believe that we are beyond change. We are not. If a bad track record determined our becoming, we would not be encouraged from Proverbs: "Keep your heart with all vigilance, for from it flow the springs of life" (Proverb 4:23).

To keep...*retain, maintain, tend, reserve, restrain, preserve, hold, stay, to have in control.* And to do so vigilantly. Sounds proactive and present to me. But why so fierce and diligent about keeping hold of our hearts?

Because it is possible to sound smooth with our tongues without consecration of our hearts. Jesus scolded the Pharisees with Isaiah's prophecy: "This people honors me with their lips, but their heart is far from me" (Matthew 15:8). He warns that such lips will worship in vain.

If you've mismanaged your heart tending and, in turn, your tongue taming, take heart: It's not too late. Jesus welcomes the regretful tongue that willingly comes to Him but sees right through the pretty tongue that willfully runs the other way.

Our God is in the business of heart transformation, and He begins anew day by day with those who are willing. Be willing, friend, stay the course, and let your redeemed heart redeem your speech. From the overflow of the heart, the mouth speaks. Lord, let our hearts overflow with You.

11

beholding
God's View of You

Everyone tells you to "just be yourself."

Unfortunately, "yourself" is not always an easy thing to discern, at least not for me. I'm 43 now, and sometimes—sometimes I'm just not sure I really know exactly who "I" am.

We look to career, age group, interests, location, ethnicity, political alliance, achievements, enneagrams, titles, or roles to define who we are.

...I'm a mom of six—boys.

...I'm Chinese.

...I'm a writer.

...I'm an artist.

...I'm a sushi lover.

To read bios and profiles online these days is to discover how many people define themselves by how they take their coffee, their job titles, or by their wildest dreams. Are we the sum of our likes, dislikes, awards, and associations?

A.W. Tozer gives us a different perspective:

What comes into our minds when we think about God is the most

143

important thing about us. The history of mankind will probably show that no people has ever risen above its religion, and man's spiritual history will positively demonstrate that no religion has ever been greater than its idea of God. Worship is pure or base as the worshiper entertains high or low thoughts of God.

For this reason the gravest question before the Church is always God Himself, and the most portentous fact about any man is not what he at a given time may say or do, but what he in his deep heart conceives God to be like.

We tend by a secret law of the soul to move toward our mental image of God. This is true not only of the individual Christian, but of the company of Christians that composes the Church. Always the most revealing thing about the Church is her idea of God.*

Allow me to restate it plainly: It doesn't so much matter what we say about God or what we do for Him; it's what we truly think about God in our most inward being that affects everything about us. We are defined by what we believe about God because who we become is directly related to what we picture in our minds when we think about Him.

- *If we picture a disappointed employer, we will think ourselves failing employees.*
- *If we envision an unjust ruler, we will act like rebellious subjects.*
- *If we see God as a genie, we will be wish makers.*
- *If we believe He is our Abba Father, we will be His children.*

Our self-esteem mirrors how we esteem God.

So here is the secret to true self-esteem: The higher we esteem—"honor" or "revere"—God for who He is, the truer our view of ourselves. When we recognize how great He is, we rightly realize how flawed we are. But when we esteem

---

* A.W. Tozer, *The Knowledge of the Holy*

Riches I heed not nor
man's empty praise
Thou mine inheritance
now and always
Thou and Thou only
first in my heart
High King of
Heaven, my
Treasure
Thou art.

God in the highest manner, we will regard the flawed souls He redeems highly as well. You see, lifting our hearts in worship to Him causes us to value who He's created us to be, in spite of imperfections. If our highly esteemed Father considers us worthy of rescue, who are we to argue and complain?

Do you feel like a nobody? Do you struggle to know *who you are*?

It's okay to be a no one to everyone if you are someone to the Holy One. Who He is in you defines who you are in Him.

Being yourself is not as important as being His.

> Be Thou my Vision, O Lord of my heart;
> Naught be all else to me, save that Thou art.
> Thou my best Thought, by day or by night,
> Waking or sleeping, Thy presence my light.
>
> Be Thou my Wisdom, and Thou my true Word;
> I ever with Thee and Thou with me, Lord;
> Thou my great Father, I Thy true son;
> Thou in me dwelling, and I with Thee one.
>
> Be Thou my battle Shield, Sword for the fight;
> Be Thou my Dignity, Thou my Delight;
> Thou my soul's Shelter, Thou my high Tow'r:
> Raise Thou me heav'nward, O Pow'r of my pow'r.
>
> Riches I heed not, nor man's empty praise,
> Thou mine Inheritance, now and always:
> Thou and Thou only, first in my heart,
> High King of Heaven, my Treasure Thou art.
>
> High King of Heaven, my victory won,
> May I reach Heaven's joys, O bright Heav'n's Sun!
> Heart of my own heart, whatever befall,
> Still be my Vision, O Ruler of all.

ELEANOR HULL, FROM A MIDDLE IRISH POEM

memorize scripture

stop condemning yourself

choose a high
view of God

rehearse your
identity in Christ

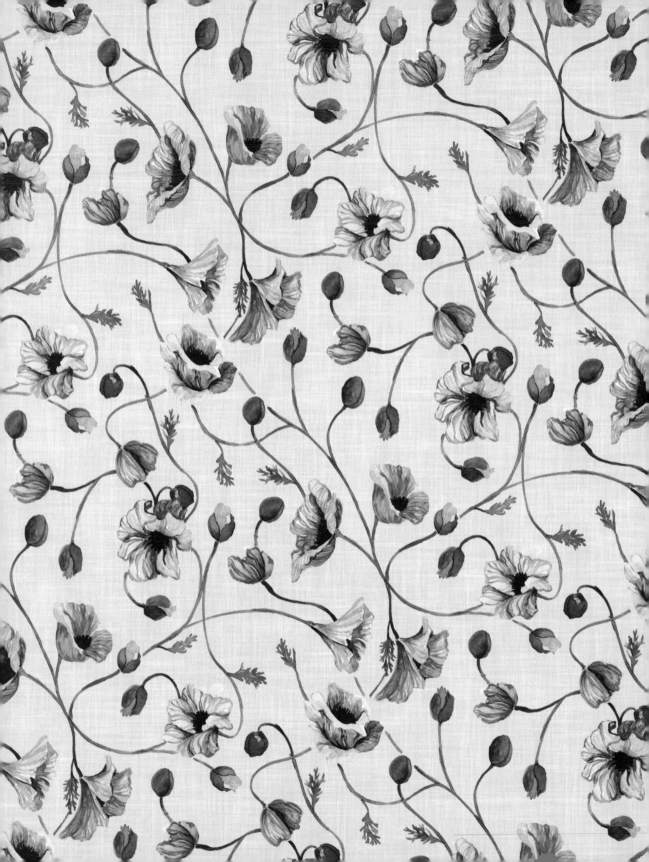

becoming

What's True About You

You can learn a lot about a woman from the contents of her purse. Some of us have hand santizer, Band-Aids, and protein bars at the ready, and some never leave home without a makeup pouch tucked in. One friend of mine carries measuring tape, and another, superglue. *You just never know what kind of day you'll have.*

Some of us are neat and organized, cleaning and sorting our purses at the end of each day, keeping careful track of what is going in and out. And then there's me and my leather tote—with my crumpled receipts, random business cards, brochures, hair ties, lipsticks, napkins with notes scrawled over them, and beloved Sunday school lesson coloring sheets stuffed into my bag after church. I'm the one who always says, "Hold on a minute—I'm sure I have a pen in here somewhere" and then proceeds to dig around for the next five minutes pulling out loose change, Hot Wheels cars, and the set of keys I lost last month instead.

The tote bag I carry is a bit like my heart and mind sometimes—packed full of potentially useful things that get misplaced or lost deep in the chaos of a hurried life.

Sometimes, when faced with my doubts, fears, and anxious thoughts, I reach for the low-hanging fruit of my own muddled thoughts and—just like shoving my hand inside my bag hoping to find a pen and emerging with a crayon instead—I come up short of what I truly need. Self-condemning lies, fearful worry, faithless complaining, and a lesser view of God are easy to settle for. Sometimes, the good things we carry get crowded out and lost in the shuffle of the junk we won't let go.

There's a Latin saying that Cicero ascribes to Bias of Priene—*Omnia mea mecum porto*—which, translated, means: "Everything I own, I carry with me." I don't think the ancients had mobile devices in mind, though it would seem so with the way we can't function without them. (Does anyone even try to remember phone numbers or birthdays anymore?) I think, instead, he meant something akin to the words of the psalmist: "I have hidden your word in my heart that I might not sin against you" (Psalm 119:11 NIV).

The psalmist forms a mental picture for me: He so treasures the Word of God that he gives it a home where it can accompany him everywhere he goes and cannot be lost, taken, or forgotten. He hides it in his heart.

I picture the rooms of his heart so taken over by truth that he is unable to entertain sin. When God's Word pushes out lies and resides in us, we will reach for truth and it will be ours to have. Can you imagine it? Rather than scrambling and digging around to find the truth about who you are and what really matters—trying to weed out the clutter to get to the good—imagine accessing the truth immediately because, more than merely available, it is *yours*.

Unlike directions, phone numbers, important dates, and account logins that we don't commit to memory, God's Word—if sifted into our memory banks and kneaded into our daily lives—becomes *ours* as we read it, study it, and hide it in our hearts. Truth, instead of being saved in a browser or stuffed in a handbag, is truly ours when it is actively in use within us.

The psalmist knew the importance not just of knowing where to find God's Word (for so many of us, on a shelf or unopened on our bedside table), but also

...put on the new self, which is being renewed in knowledge after the image of its Creator.

COLOSSIANS 3:10

IN CHRIST, I AM...

forgiven
EPHESIANS 1:7

His child
JOHN 1:12

free
ROMANS 8:2

loved
COLOSSIANS 3:12

made new
2 CORINTHIANS 5:17

joint heir with Christ
ROMANS 8:17

chosen
EPHESIANS 1:4

a citizen of heaven
PHILIPPIANS 3:20

set apart
1 CORINTHIANS 1:30

lacking nothing
PHILIPPIANS 4:19

of how to hide it deeply in his heart. He uses 176 verses in Psalm 119 to extol the excellencies of God and His statutes. He is motivated by love, obedience, and worship. He doesn't want to be caught without it lest he miss the mark without the map.

My husband, Troy, often says (and he's right), "The clearest evidence that we possess something is that we are possessed by it."

We can't use what we don't have, and we don't have what's not ours. Who we become day by day is shaped by what we can't live without as we go. Dear believer, let's travel light, carrying only what is true and worthy of possessing.

12

beholding
God's Goodness at the Table

t may come as a surprise to anyone who's known me for some time, but I had almost no cooking skills when I first became a wife. I remember (to my embarrassment) how fascinated I was with Hamburger Helper because I had not yet understood how to cook from scratch or *how* they made that box mix so mysteriously tasty. Then, slowly but surely, I fell in love with serving a home-cooked meal to a table of guests. Those were the days before readily accessible online recipe archives, when aspiring cooks dog-eared magazines and smudged cookbook pages with molten lava cake batter. I couldn't wait to try out new techniques (brown butter!), discover new ingredients (crème fraîche!), or refer to a simple mixture of carrots, onions, and celery as *mirepoix*. So fancy. The skies of the culinary world opened up, and the savory seas of homemade chicken stock parted; I was smitten with the kitchen.

So, who then was that woman yesterday afternoon who stood in front of my refrigerator and bemoaned yet another meal that needed prepping for the seven guys who live in my house? There is a difference between culinary curiosity and

consistently serving meals day in and day out at the table. One showcases skill and amuses the palate, and the other—while able to do the same—is most often a display of dedication, perseverance, and sacrifice.

The children of Israel understood something of repetition with no end in sight. Just three days after God performed one of the most memorable and powerful acts in the Bible—the parting of the Red Sea—through which His people had safe passage and rescue, these same children began to complain, fearing the lack of water and food in the desert. How often we're wowed by God's goodness, only to find ourselves moaning about persevering in it. God had delivered the Israelites from slavery and promised them their own home—a land flowing with milk and honey—but first He led them out into the desert for 40 years to show them who He was and how He would provide for them.

God had limitless options for providing food for his people, but He chose to demonstrate His provision one day at a time—no more and no less. He wanted His children to anticipate His faithfulness, to receive it, to gather it, to feast from it, and to repeat that process the very next day, breaking only for the Sabbath.

> Behold, I am about to rain bread from heaven for you, and the people shall go out and gather a day's portion every day, that I may test them, whether they will walk in my law or not...At evening you shall know that it was the Lord who brought you out of the land of Egypt, and in the morning you shall see the glory of the Lord, because he has heard your grumbling against the Lord.
>
> Exodus 16:4,6-7

Most of us don't grumble in our spirit because we lack food (as we throw out unused groceries that have gone bad), but because we lack gratitude. The Israelites were the same—their grumbling did not ultimately reveal their fear of hunger as much as their faulty focus. Their faithful God miraculously made a way for their rescue, but they could only see their empty stomachs. Our God graciously makes it possible for us to not just dine but dine with pleasure, yet so

You Shall Know that it was the Lord

Behold I stand at the door and knock. If anyone hears my voice and opens the door, I will come in to him and eat with him and and him, he with Me.

REVELATION 3:20

often we fixate on what it takes for us to gather. We miss the provision when we don't behold the Provider.

That we might "know it was the LORD" who sustained us in times of famine and plenty—*this* is the reason we gather, serve, and feast day by day. Friend, your faithfulness to take what He's given and remind your household to take and eat has nothing to do with crème fraîche or mirepoix; we can feast on beans and rice or steak tartare...because the Lord provides it and we've been given the opportunity to taste and see that He is good.

TASTE AND SEE

serve store-bought donuts

open your doo

meet your neighbor

spontaneously make room for guests

invite a guest without putting laundry away

becoming

Share the Feast

e recently discovered a new-to-us favorite sushi restaurant in the little town we moved to. Troy and I tried it out on a date and were amazed that such artistic flavor pairings and presentation could exist apart from the big city. We came home from our date and told the kids—also sushi lovers—about our experience. We described our meal, told them about the wild pairing of slices of apple-pear with hamachi, and pronounced the experience "life changing" in the dramatic way foodies sometimes do.

They nodded, raised their eyebrows, and were happy for us. But it wasn't until a few weeks later, on a half-off happy hour night, when they experienced it for themselves. No longer taking our word for it, the sushi was real to them.

I sometimes think about the table of hospitality the same way. People who are invited in and given a seat at our tables observe and receive relationship, provision, nurturing, and welcome in a way no mere invitation to church can provide. Instead of handing someone information about Jesus or an invitation to Easter service, or telling them that the gospel is life changing, we give them the opportunity to experience it through our hospitality.

So much of Jesus' ministry was done at the table. The wedding feast at Cana, the feeding of the 5,000 and the 4,000, the meal with Levi the tax collector, and the last supper with His disciples—these are just a few examples that gave rise to the reputation of Jesus that "the Son of Man has come eating and drinking" (Luke 7:34). Was Jesus a foodie, or did He simply recognize that there are 21 opportunities every week for us to extend welcome and friendship, meet a need, and serve up the soul-satisfying fare of God's grace?

Do you feel reluctant or unequipped to offer hospitality? God's Word addresses our concerns by turning our gaze to His provisions:

Worried about a messy, in-progress home?

> And I am sure of this, that he who began a good work in you will bring it to completion at the day of Jesus Christ.
>
> PHILIPPIANS 1:6

Unsure how to be a friend?

> No longer do I call you servants, for the servant does not know what his master is doing; but I have called you friends, for all that I have heard from my Father I have made known to you.
>
> JOHN 15:15

Afraid you're not a good cook?

> I am the bread of life. Whoever comes to me will never go hungry, and whoever believes in me will never be thirsty.
>
> JOHN 6:35 NIV

The pressure's off, friends. We don't need to be chefs extraordinaire, inspiring homemakers, or decadent entertainers. We simply need to put our love for Jesus on display in the ordinary places of our daily lives. You can't get a more consistently ordinary context than three meals a day on a scratched and well-worn kitchen table. But the fare that one might taste there? If it's served up in Jesus' name, it will be a feast indeed.

13

beholding
God's Mercy When Things Seem Unfair

The winding path between contentment and discontentment is a well-worn, familiar road in my heart. I know its bends and switchbacks. I anticipate its potholes and know where I'll trip if I drag my feet each time I walk that road. For me, contentment in the day to day is as elusive as a perfectly fitting pair of jeans—always promising but rarely keeping its shape. As soon as I think I have the perfect conditions for contentment, things change...or *I* change.

At best, discontentment is a pacing back and forth of someone who's itching for better; at worst, it's the bitter, defiant stomping of someone when "better" isn't given. Turns out, it's fairly simple to diagnose the source of 99 percent of our unhappiness. We can point to unmet expectations, relationships that end in broken hearts, that thing *he said*, or that thing *she did*. We can pin our unhappiness on endless circumstances gone wrong, but the inconvenient truth is that our

greatest everyday unhappiness stems from the error of believing we deserve—are entitled to—better, and that God must be holding out on us.

Discontentment is the weed that grows up through the cracks of our disbelief or *wrong* belief. Cracks might show up in different places in your life, but I'm guessing they look similar to mine:

The wrong belief that...

- *...if God really cared, He'd right the wrongs against me*
- *...things should be easier for those of us who do right*
- *...I should have what she has*
- *...progress should come quicker*
- *...if others really knew me, I'd have all the relationships I truly crave*
- *...my hard work should guarantee fruitfulness*

Honest self-examination is brutal but revealing.

Sometimes things appear to be unfair or unjust, and they stoke our bitterness. We struggle to humbly receive, but instead secretly demand. Jesus told the parable of the Prodigal Son in Luke 15. It's a familiar story with a sobering reminder. It illustrates welcome and mercy from a loving Father, but it equally warns against becoming a self-righteous rule follower. We identify with the prodigal son as Jesus receives us in spite of our waywardness, but it's the older brother that we so often resemble in our self-reliant pride and discontent.

> Now his older son was in the field, and as he came and drew near to the house, he heard music and dancing. And he called one of the servants and asked what these things meant. And he said to him, "Your brother has come, and your father has killed the fattened calf, because he has received him back safe and sound." But he was angry and refused to go in. His father came out and entreated him, but he answered his father, "Look, these many years I have served you, and I never disobeyed your command, yet

Behold what manner of love the father has given to us, that we should be called children of God. And that is what we are!

1 John 3:1

you never gave me a young goat, that I might celebrate with my friends. But when this son of yours came, who has devoured your property with prostitutes, you killed the fattened calf for him!" And he said to him, "Son, you are always with me, and all that is mine is yours. It was fitting to celebrate and be glad, for this your brother was dead, and is alive; he was lost, and is found."

Luke 15:25-32

Jesus' parables were illustrative, not prescriptive. The father's response to a self-righteous, entitled son—bitter, believing he deserved better—illustrates our Father's response to our sinful pride: He puts His love on display and tells us to behold His great mercy: "Son, you are always with me, and all that is mine is yours." Fixing our eyes on His mercy takes the wind out of entitlement and discontent. His grace causes us to see ourselves truthfully: undeserving of His relentless love and lavish generosity. His great mercy fills the cracks of our unbelief and—when received—allows little room for bitterness and discontentment to spring up.

See what kind of love the Father has given to us, that we should be called children of God; and so we are.

1 John 3:1

That path between discontentment and contentment may still be familiar, but it can become less worn when we stay fixed on how merciful the Father is to welcome us home. When we stop looking over our shoulder, peering into the future, tallying up and comparing notes from our left and right...and instead, behold the amazing grace of our Father, we move ever closer to true contentment and grateful praise for what He has done and all that He's given.

bitterness & pride are your
real enemies

think on god's
mercy

preach to
yourself

run to comfort
in Christ

hope in God

examine
yourself

becoming

Remember Your Purpose

clutched my chest and sat up in my bed frantically. It was still the dark hours of the night, but I was suddenly wide awake...anxious, burdened, angry. It wasn't a heart attack that woke me; it was heart*ache*—heartache so severe it would continue to wake me each night for weeks to come during that difficult season. I remember that spring as though it was yesterday. I had never known such hurt and devastation in my adult life—the kind of pain that leaves you wondering how truth can be so elusive and circumstances can turn out so seemingly unfair despite good intentions. Perhaps you've known a similar season.

Following Jesus does not spare us from sleepless nights, unjust circumstances, or silent cries into our pillows. Following Jesus promises us comfort in the midst of those earthly trials and hope that all wrongs will be made right in the end by God, who can be trusted:

> He will wipe every tear from their eyes, and death shall be no more,
> neither shall there be mourning, nor crying, nor pain anymore,

for the former things have passed away..."Behold, I am making all things new."

REVELATION 21:4-5

But what about today? What about right now—in the middle of answers that don't make sense and outcomes that seem unjust? How do we put off bitterness in unjust circumstances and put on hope in God's sovereignty?

We have an example in David as the Bible follows the course of his life. Anointed king, chosen by God, demonstrating righteous character as a young man, yet David spent years hiding and running from Saul on account of the reigning king's jealousy and rage. David was promised the kingdom, and yet he waited years for the throne and for wrongs to be made right. David was a man who knew how it felt to be attacked, hunted, betrayed, abandoned, and weary...all while seeking to obey the Lord:

> My heart is in anguish within me; the terrors of death have fallen upon me. Fear and trembling come upon me, and horror over-whelms me...
>
> For it is not an enemy who taunts me—then I could bear it; it is not an adversary who deals insolently with me—then I could hide from him. But it is you, a man, my equal, my companion, my familiar friend. We used to take sweet counsel together; within God's house we walked in the throng.

PSALM 55:4-5,12-14

David was no stranger to the unfair, unjust, and unexpectedly hurtful. He knew what it was to be betrayed by someone he trusted...to have the rug pulled out from under him...to be on the run when he was supposed to have a place at the table. Yet he hoped in the Lord in the midst of his very real circumstances by reminding himself who God was and why God was his comfort.

During a trip to Israel recently, I crawled into the remote and hidden cave of Adullam where David sought refuge from Saul. I marveled at sitting in the very

This is my Father's world. O let me ne'er forget that though the wrong seems oft so strong, God is the Ruler Yet. This is my Father's world: Why should my heart be sad? The Lord is King; let the heavens ring! God reigns; Let the earth be glad!

place where David penned Psalm 57 as his heart turned from fear and desperation to assurance and praise:

> Be merciful to me, O God, be merciful to me, for in you my soul takes refuge; in the shadow of your wings I will take refuge, till the storms of destruction pass by. I cry out to God Most High, to God who fulfills his purpose for me. He will send from heaven and save me; he will put to shame him who tramples on me. God will send out his steadfast love and his faithfulness!
>
> Psalm 57:1-3

Heartaches can either mold us into confident worshippers or defensive doubters. Who we become in the wrestling of them is not neutral. The shape we take depends on where we find refuge in disappointment and the unexpected. David chose to direct his heart and mind to the faithfulness of God and His purposes, combating his disbelief by preaching truth to himself. It's as if he knew that it's more dangerous to turn our hearts away from God than to be on the run from an enemy.

Today, as we face the very circumstances that *shouldn't be*, remember: We aren't promised answers that heal, outcomes we think we deserve, or timing that makes the most sense to us. Instead, we are promised that in every circumstance, God's purposes will prevail and will not be thwarted by manipulators, liars, or cheats. (Maybe that both comforts and convicts you, as it does me.) Injustice and selfish schemes are no match for Him who wastes nothing: "We know that in all things God works for the good of those who love him, who have been called according to his purpose" (Romans 8:28 NIV).

14

beholding

Worship Follows Mercy

ur hands are storytellers.

Rugged, weathered hands—calloused from gripping an ax handle—tell of long hours under a relentless sun and through the winter cold. They tell of diligence, season after season. Then there are my own—unmanicured, with torn cuticles that betray an anxious season of habits of forgetfulness, taking the intense focus of this season out on my nails. If you close your eyes, I bet you're able recall the touch, the scent, the peculiarities of your mom's or grandma's hands. You might look across the table and read a bit of someone's life story in their hands. Our bodies have a way of saying things our lips don't.

Our bodies show the wear and tear of the lives we live. No matter how many miracle creams we use, supplements we take, or exercises we perform, there is no changing our body's trajectory toward deterioration. In a world that spins on the axis of physical beauty and ability, the good news of Jesus redeems our distorted view of our own bodies—saggy, broken, wrinkly, used up, and imperfect as they are—and gives us purpose that doesn't depend on physical attractiveness or achievement. This is *good news,* amen?

The apostle Paul, perhaps the greatest missionary who ever lived, lets us in on how others perceived him in his letter to the Corinthians: "They say, 'His letters are weighty and strong, but his bodily presence is weak, and his speech of no account'" (2 Corinthians 10:10). I don't know about you, but this review of Paul gives me hope. It reminds me I have nothing to prove, nothing to boast in, and nothing to give but Christ in me.

This same Paul penned the letter to the Romans, in which the first 11 chapters spell out the unmistakable mercy of God in redemption through Christ. We're shown the full picture of what we who are in Christ are saved from, what we are saved to, and where we place our hope as we live in the newness of redemption. Paul then turns and brings into view the entirety of all the mercies of God he's unpacked for the 11 previous chapters and shares this familiar verse:

> Therefore, I urge you, brothers and sisters, in view of God's mercy, to offer your bodies as a living sacrifice, holy and pleasing to God—this is your true and proper worship.
>
> Romans 12:1 niv

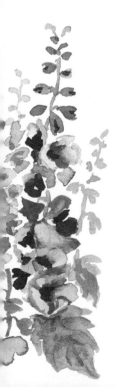

When we read this verse, we tend to immediately focus on *our part*—our duty. We put "offer your bodies as a living sacrifice" on the checklist of "true and proper" things to get after on our journey to holiness. But if this offering were dependent on how fit, how strong, how pretty, or how capable we were, true worship would escape the likes of Paul, you, and me.

Paul makes it clear that it is by grace that we are saved—that we can offer our bodies at all. It's the gracious mercy of God that rescued us from a life of self worship to a life of true worship. *Therefore,* when we behold God's mercy, we respond with our bodies to what has begun first in our hearts: holy reverence for a faithful God. Our checklists get us nowhere with a God who demands more than we could ever accomplish and satisfies all the requirements Himself on our behalf. That *is* good news.

DO NOT CONFORM TO THE PATTERN OF THIS WORLD, BUT BE TRANSFORMED BY THE RENEWING OF YOUR MIND.

ROMANS 12:2

For the Lord sees not as man sees; man looks on the outward appearance, but the Lord looks on the heart.

1 SAMUEL 16:7

God is more glorified when our broken hearts and weathered hands match in true worship than when glossy declarations of our lips and big displays of our religiosity make more of our own physical resources than of His mercy. Our offerings—big and small, feeble bodies and strong—will always begin with our heart worship. That's where the Lord sets His gaze: "The LORD sees not as man sees: man looks on the outward appearance, but the LORD looks on the heart" (1 Samuel 16:7).

So, for the young and old, the flabby and strong, the in shape and in progress, the ones who turn heads or the ones who disappear in a crowd: God sees you. He receives you as you are.

Take your eyes off of your physical weaknesses and imperfections, friends, and set your eyes on the great view of God's mercy, again and again. The perfect offering has already been given in Jesus (He was the spotless lamb). You and I are welcomed, blemishes and all, because the good news of redemption will always be our *why* in worship and our *how* in offering up our lives.

break an old pattern by
savoring something
better

establish a new
pattern

meet with
Jesus every day
for the next 30 days

becoming

Form a Pattern with Posture and Practice

There is a pattern to a waltz. Even when the music is inaudible, the one-two-three, one-two-three rhythm of two people waltzing across the dance floor is unmistakable to an observer. The same could be said of a jive, swing, or salsa. We recognize a dance by the pattern of its dancer.

That's what comes to mind when I read the next verse in Paul's instruction to the Romans about looking to the mercy of God and responding by offering themselves as living sacrifices:

Do not be conformed to this world, but be transformed by the renewal of your mind, that by testing you may discern what is the will of God, what is good and acceptable and perfect.

ROMANS 12:2

As with a waltz, posture and practice define the pattern in a Christ-follower's life. Posture is the position, stance, or approach to something, and practice is the fleshing out of that posture. Our posture as believers is that of grateful recipients of the mercies of God—we look back at all He's done and move forward in a posture of praise. Practice makes a posture become a pattern. The conforming that Paul speaks about in Romans 12 can be to our benefit or destruction; it is a process of making small adjustments repeatedly, practicing a pattern over and over until it no longer feels foreign or distasteful. Our appetites change with exposure and savoring. Daily savoring of sin will conform us to the world just as daily savoring of God's Word by the Spirit will conform us to Christ. Paul instructs us to break the pattern of casually becoming like the world by intentionally renewing our minds with a Christlike pattern.

Sometimes we're surprised when our desire for holiness grows cold, our pursuit of God wanes, and our likeness to the world catches up with us. But it shouldn't take us by surprise if we are not intentionally and continually renewing our minds with the Word of God. We do not passively become wise in discernment or worshipful in our everyday lives, and we don't automatically become living sacrifices without a deliberate choice to respond to His love with obedience. A new pattern takes time to establish and grows when love—not duty—is our motivator. As the old hymn reveals, "Love will make obedience sweet."*

How, then, do we love God, and in turn, grow to be more like Him? My friend Jen Wilkin puts it this way: "The heart cannot love what the mind does not know." Our minds, renewed in and by the Word, direct our hearts...and our hearts, in turn, affect who we *become*:

- *We choose a posture of humble gratitude and turn to God's Word.*
- *We practice that posture again and again.*
- *We begin to see a pattern of the wisdom and worship* Paul speaks of in Romans 12:1-2.

When we place our full trust in Jesus, we are instantly forgiven and made right with God, but sanctification is the process of *becoming*—day by day—through the work of Christ in our lives. That new pattern is an outward transformation that reveals inward change. It takes time. It takes God. It takes posture and practice. For all this and more, He is faithful: God loves us just as we are...while He loves us *into* who we will become.

---

* Joseph Swain, 1792, "Come, Ye Souls by Sin Afflicted."

the heart cannot
LOVE
what the mind
does not
KNOW.

· JEN WILKIN ·

15

beholding

Rest Is Productive

hen our third man cub was four years old, we experienced a year of him unexplainably waking throughout the night, screaming and crying. Troy and I (mostly Troy because he's a very kind husband) would be in and out of bed seven or eight times a night that entire year, trying to console a little boy who couldn't fully explain whether the problem was pain, fear, or something else. As a young mom at the time with three other boys, two older and one toddler, I was exhausted and exasperated. After a few months of trying everything and feeling incredibly worn out, Troy suddenly started getting up early again each morning, despite sleepless nights. I still remember my disbelief (and a bit of defensiveness) when he told me he was getting up before the kids to read his Bible and spend time with the Lord: "That's great, babe, but how in the world can you afford to get less sleep?" His answer will perennially be a favorite reminder: "Honey...I can't afford *not* to."

Troy knew what he couldn't live without, and that has been a significant reminder to me as I make priority choices every day. In that season, I equated

195

survival with another few hours of sleep, but Troy looked to spiritual rest in the Lord as the means to thrive.

Time with the Lord is not a magic pill, not a formula, not a duty, certainly not an "easy button," and not akin to burning incense to appease a distant god; it's simply what we're created for—a relationship with Him. Functioning apart from the fuel of His presence is like taking a cross-country road trip with an empty gas tank. It brings to mind another story of one who chose time with the Lord, and one who chose what seemed more "productive"—the familiar account of Mary and Martha hosting Jesus in Martha's home:

> Now as they went on their way, Jesus entered a village. And a woman named Martha welcomed him into her house. And she had a sister called Mary, who sat at the Lord's feet and listened to his teaching. But Martha was distracted with much serving. And she went up to him and said, "Lord, do you not care that my sister has left me to serve alone? Tell her then to help me." But the Lord answered her, "Martha, Martha, you are anxious and troubled about many things, but one thing is necessary. Mary has chosen the good portion, which will not be taken away from her."
>
> LUKE 10:38-42

Perhaps, like Martha, in our task-mindedness, we forget that rest—ceasing from work and being still before the Lord—is not a luxury; rest *is* productive.

How often I look at the mess in my home, the incomplete home projects, the tables to be set, the meals to be made, the shelves to be dusted...and roll my eyes at the idea of rest (or anyone who might suggest it). But God Himself, who rested after six days of creating the heavens and the earth, didn't set the example for rest to simply give us a break but rather to *be* our rest.

Like Martha, we spin and toil anxiously over "many things," and often forget to choose the portion that is most necessary. We think it a luxury to rest because we think everything depends on us. The Martha mindset puts my own abilities and resources on center stage, but a Mary posture looks to Jesus.

one
thing
is
Necessary

Better is one day in Your courts than a thousand elsewhere.

PSALM 84:10

James 1:23-24 (NIV) reminds us that it's not the "doing" that is the issue but what drives our faithfulness:

> Anyone who listens to the word but does not do what it says is like someone who looks at his face in a mirror and, after looking at himself, goes away and immediately forgets what he looks like.

Being a "doer" is putting into action our heart posture. All the productivity and perseverance we strive for find their fuel in our perspective on true rest. When we see how much we're provided for in Christ, we can be fruitful for His glory *because* He's fruitful *in* us, and we can rest because His rest is productive.

In our present cultural glorification of busy, we can choose to see our to-do lists, calendars, and schedules differently. It's not that Jesus didn't expect work to be done, meals to be made, and tables to be set; He simply called Martha to recognize opportunity for best in the midst of all that was good. All work, no matter how needed and useful, becomes anxious toiling if not fueled by our most-needed sustenance: rest in the Lord.

The psalmist says it this way:

> Better is one day in your courts than a thousand elsewhere; I would rather be a doorkeeper in the house of my God than dwell in the tents of the wicked.
>
> PSALM 84:10 NIV

- *Rest is where we remember that He is God and we are not.*
- *Rest is where we remember that He holds all things together without our help.*
- *Rest is where we remember that God created the time restraints and limitations we rebel against.*
- *Rest is where we remember that He is at work in us, even in the waiting.*

We might think we can't afford to take time for rest, but really, we can't afford *not* to.

schedule rest

close your computer

prioritize heart
over hustle

leave blank space on the calendar

sit still

becoming
Stop Making Bricks

hether we realize it or not, we are bound bricklayers by birth. All day, every day, we gather straw, make bricks, meet the quota, and try to perform to the standard. We relate to the Israelites, enslaved in Egypt (Exodus 5—read it if you haven't lately), more than we know. Work and productivity are ceaseless taskmasters, no matter what kind of work surrounds us. The drive for more, better, faster, or higher numbers is not a modern ailment unique to a world where the World Wide Web never sleeps. Before the people of God ever stepped into the Promised Land, they had known generations of endless work under the heavy hand of the Egyptians. We read the account of their burdens and follow their journey to freedom and rest, but somehow we so easily miss the parallels in our own lives:

- *The basket of laundry waits to be folded...*
- *There are dishes in the sink...*
- *E-mails are waiting in the inbox...*
- *Home projects are half complete...*

- *That conversation has not been resolved…*
- *The decision is still not made…*

It's hard to make room for rest when there's more work to be done.

Perhaps we look around at our self-generated pace of life and wonder if this is what our loving Father had in mind when He made the earth to complete one rotation in 24 hours?

Maybe, like me, you've become painfully aware as you look at your life: *Cutting corners on rest doesn't get you ahead.*

But it's not productivity in itself that enslaves us (the Bible warns against idleness!). It's the idolizing of productivity and the freedom we think it promises if we only perform to an unobtainable standard that drives the whip.

In the same way the taskmasters of ancient Egypt continually demanded more and kept the Israelites bound to an endless cycle of fear and striving, our addiction to work (even good work) without rest is bondage to a self-centered resistance of God's sufficient grace and rescue. God offered freedom and a way off the hamster wheel of performance through Himself:

> I have heard the groaning of the people of Israel whom the Egyptians hold as slaves, and I have remembered my covenant. Say therefore to the people of Israel, "I am the Lord, and I will bring you out from under the burdens of the Egyptians, and I will deliver you from slavery to them, and I will redeem you with an outstretched arm and with great acts of judgment. I will take you to be my people, and I will be your God, and you shall know that I am the Lord your God, who has brought you out from under the burdens of the Egyptians."
>
> Exodus 6:5-7

God did not arbitrarily lead His people out of Egypt and into the Promised Land via 40 years in the wilderness; it was a purposeful picture of redemption we would later know fully through the cross…through Jesus. The Lord commanded

forming

REST IS PRODUCTIVE.

and demonstrated rest for His people to show us our limitations and His sufficient provision to take care of futile striving once and for all.

When we don't rest, when we don't set the work aside, when we don't stop making bricks even though a way through the desert to the Promised Land is offered to us through Jesus, we live as slaves to the burden of sin rather than freed children in Christ.

The writer of Hebrews in the New Testament draws the connection for us:

> So then, there remains a Sabbath rest for the people of God, for whoever has entered God's rest has also rested from his works as God did from his. Let us therefore strive to enter that rest, so that no one may fall by the same sort of disobedience.
>
> HEBREWS 4:9-11

Has staying ahead of the game in all areas of your life become a normal pattern for survival? Have you forgotten that though you're a bound bricklayer by birth, you're now a freed child of God through redemption?

It's a simple reminder we all need: We weren't made for 30-hour days when God only gave us 24. We weren't designed for self-sufficiency when God created us to need a Savior. We can set aside all our tools for building our own kingdoms and rest in Him who invites and equips us to be a part of His. Rest is for the ones who stop running, stop fighting, stop trying to scrounge up enough straw to be pleasing to their master. When we surrender our own brick-making tools and go with Jesus, God, through Christ, is already pleased with you and me. There's no building better or higher or faster that will endear you to Him. All He asks is for us to lay down our bricks and rest in Him.

16

beholding
Our True Home

Home. All the hopes and hurts, longings and ideas of love—all wrapped up in one single word. We fluff our nests, repaint our walls, and build roofs over our heads. We long for home. We leave the party early, kick off our heels, and change into our favorite old sweatpants at home. We eat peanut butter straight from the jar with a spoon at home. We cry tears no one sees when we come back home. Be it a dorm room or a farmhouse, home is much less about location than it is about where we find rest. But no matter how much we make our house a home, invest in a dream property, or finally surround ourselves with the things and the people we love, there's still a nagging realization deep in our bones every day that we're simply *not home yet.*

I resonate with these words from C.S. Lewis, maybe even more so now as a grown woman who's developed a career, raised a beautiful family, remodeled homes, purchased desired furniture, acquired some acreage, invested in communities. What seemed to be *everything* I could dream of as a young woman fails to fully satisfy now.

If we find ourselves with a desire that nothing in the world can satisfy, the most probable explanation is that we were made for another world.

No amount of finding our place here on earth will satisfy the longing we have to find our place *with Him.* We can stop looking frantically to our past, our future, our left or right to feel fully at home—we won't find it here on this dusty earth.

So this is the perennial reminder my heart needs: *I was made for another world, but given a specific amount of time, things, and people to carefully steward and bring along as I journey home.* Steward well and travel light. Not feeling quite at home is the very thing God uses to draw us to abide with Him.

> Jesus answered him, "If anyone loves me, he will keep my word, and my Father will love him, and we will come to him and make our home with him."
>
> JOHN 14:23

Do you see? God chooses to make *His* home with *us* when He invites us to abide in Him. It's a home of intimate belonging and a place of security that doesn't fluctuate with the market, upkeep, or resources. It's a home we can't lose, a longing we can't fill otherwise. We can't buy it, rent it, or earn this home; we're simply given the keys when we humbly ask Him to simply *move in.* Abiding in Christ is our key to making our home *with* Christ.

This journey we've been on to discover the art of everyday worship—to behold God's faithfulness and become transformed to His likeness day by day—is not so that we might be more at home here on earth, but so that we might travel with our true home in view and securely in our hearts. We needn't live as wandering sojourners, orphans, or gypsies. We need not be nervous tenants worried about an eviction notice. We may have no abiding city here, but we belong to a true home whose welcome never ends for those who enter in. We may still know longing, this side of heaven, but if home is Christ *with* us, rest and "welcome home" is continually before us, wherever we go.

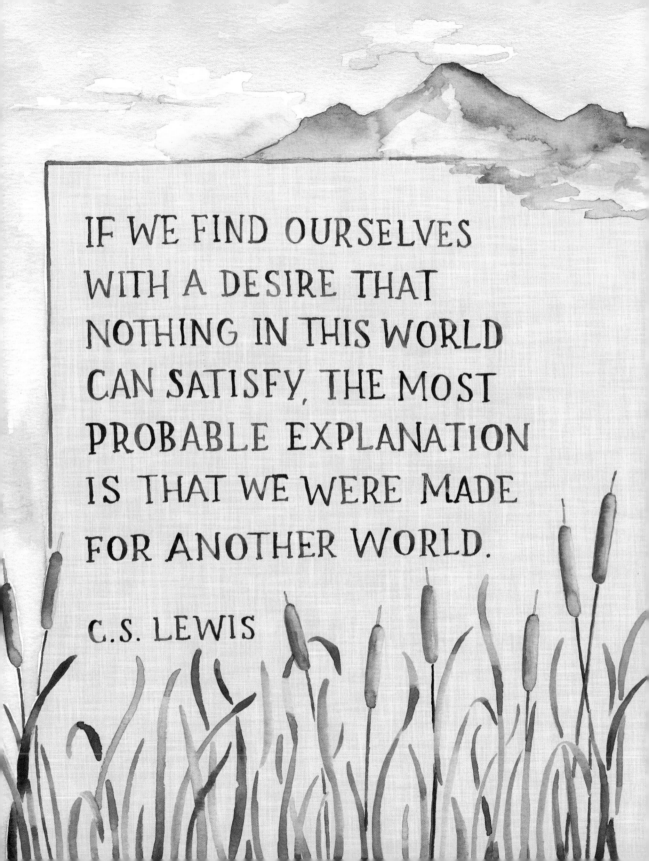

IF WE FIND OURSELVES WITH A DESIRE THAT NOTHING IN THIS WORLD CAN SATISFY, THE MOST PROBABLE EXPLANATION IS THAT WE WERE MADE FOR ANOTHER WORLD.

C.S. LEWIS

how
has god kept you
close to Himself?

describe
your
heavenly
home

fight to abide

make a list of the
places you've
lived

becoming
Actively Abide

e bought a property with a pond a few years ago in western Colorado. We were so excited, but by the first summer of owning the property, we discovered that the pond isn't spring fed and dries up completely each year because it is filled up only once annually when irrigation waters are released. It looked so full and so promising and boasted of lakeside picnics, but alas, *it's not a real pond.* It's not connected to a source that continually supplies it...a source that doesn't run out. If you come in the summer, our pond is actually just a big hole in the ground.

Our pond reminds me of the language used throughout the apostle John's letters in the New Testament on the issue of abiding. Just as a pond must be supplied and connected to an active source in order for it to remain, so must we abide in Christ as believers. There is action involved in abiding. We tend to think of abiding as sweetly passive, but John describes it as anything but:

> As the Father has loved me, so have I loved you. Abide in my love.
> If you keep my commandments, you will abide in my love, just
> as I have kept my Father's commandments and abide in his love.
>
> JOHN 15:9-10

The meaning of the original Greek word *meno*, which is translated as "abide" in the New Testament, means *to stay, to remain, to be true to, to persevere, to keep walking beside, to get in close, to dwell, to be near, to not perish, to withstand.*

It means to physically stand your ground. It means not to wander away or give up your resolve. It means to stay engaged and endure. It means to keep in step with Christ and not yield to the world.

Abiding is active—it's a choice, and it doesn't happen passively. Abiding may sound like a gentle concept, but John writes, throughout his teachings, that abiding is a deliberate pursuit—one that's costly, causes us to discern, assures us in the midst of doubt, and keeps us persevering with Christ and with one another as we walk lightly—aliens in a foreign land.

And here's my real-life definition: If home is where the heart is, then *what we love determines where we will be most steadfast.* Abiding is loving Jesus above all else so that we find no other place to be than by His side.

- *Social media will not feel like home.*
- *A bigger house will not feel like home.*
- *Secret sins will not feel like home.*
- *Titles, degrees, and status will not feel like home.*
- *Addictions and controlling habits will not feel like home.*

Though we often place our focus on keeping His commandments, worrying that we aren't doing everything we're supposed to, John reminds us that abiding in His love and keeping His commandments go hand in hand. We can't follow Him apart from being led by His love for us.

No one who abides in Christ *keeps on sinning* (1 John 3:6) because when we abide, we *keep on loving* Christ first. We can't simultaneously do both. If we're busy rehearsing truth and practicing nearness to the presence of God, we won't have bandwidth to practice perfecting the pattern of sin. There's no room to be enamored by the penthouse of sin when our every need is met in our home with Christ.

HOMEWARD

Abide with me,
fast falls the
eventide; the
darkness deepens
Lord with me abide.
When other helpers
fail and comforts
flee, Help of the
helpless, O
abide with me.

HENRY FRANCIS LYTE

Maybe you've spent so much energy looking for home in the comforts and temporary fixes this world has to offer that you've forgotten that you were made to abide. Not to remain by keeping up. Not to be steadied by success. Not to find shelter in appearances—like that pond on my property, looking filled up and eager to welcome boats and fish and ducks but running dry because it isn't connected to a steady water source. A pond that doesn't remain supplied with fresh water is a pond that won't ultimately sustain life. And so it is with us.

Actively choosing to stay in close and press in when it's hard is our safeguard in times of temptation, self-condemnation, fear, and doubt. Active abiders aren't perfect followers of Jesus; they are *practicing* followers of Christ, supplied by living water, connected to the source. For the homeward bound, abiding is actively purposing to persevere in Jesus as He actively purposes to never let us go.

And we all, with unveiled face, beholding the glory of the Lord, are being transformed into the same image from one degree of glory to another. For this comes from the Lord who is the Spirit.

2 CORINTHIANS 3:18

DEAR FRIEND,

You are in the process of *becoming*. Every day is an opportunity to be shaped and formed by what moves your heart...drives your thoughts...captures your gaze. Is it any wonder, then, that what you behold matters in your day-to-day? My prayer is that these pages have caused you to see your everyday a little differently—to see it as God sees it: an opportunity to demonstrate His love and His faithfulness in your circumstances.

We become what we behold when we set our hearts and minds on Christ and His redemption story right in the midst of our daily lives. Not just on Sunday, not just on holidays, not just when extraordinarily hard or wonderful things happen...but *today*.

The more we behold and treasure Him, the more we become like Him and see His purposes in our circumstances. We are transformed as we walk with Him. The most ordinary days become extraordinary places of transformation when we hope in Christ instead of our circumstances. So, friend, lean in. We can worship God—*praise, adore, rejoice, hope, rest, exalt, and honor Him*—right where we are. No circumstance is too ordinary or too forgotten for God to meet us there in worship. His transforming grace turns our "everyday ordinary" into a holy place of *becoming*.

Cheering you on as we walk with Him,

Ruth

ACKNOWLEDGMENTS

This book is an offering, supported by so many hands—far more than this page will hold. But my heartfelt gratitude goes out to these, the midwives of this labor of love:

Christ, the One worthy of *all* worship—thank You for drawing me near and making Yourself known in our everyday.

Troy, who lives out humble worship and persistent praise in seen and unseen ways every day—you inspire me, my love.

Caleb, Liam, Stone, Judah, Asa, and Haddon—thank you, boys, for cheering your mama on daily.

Betty—thank you for being not only an excellent editor but an excellent friend.

Janelle—thank you for so carefully shaping this book with your creative sense and enthusiasm. I'm so grateful we're so in sync with each other (on more than just amazing Asian eats).

Eve, Gina, Shanelle, Sarah, Rachael, Finn, and Caleb—I couldn't ask for a more dedicated, Christ-honoring team to carry the work and mission of GraceLaced, Inc. Thank you for cheering me on, giving grace, filling in, putting in the hours, persevering season after season, and reminding me continually why we get to do the work we do. You all are the literal best.

Sarah—thank you for investing your artistry into everything GraceLaced, Inc., but especially into this book, whose pages quietly tell of your dedication and creativity.

Ruth—thank you for being an integral part of my journey; I could not be here without your friendship, spunk, and diligence. I smile at all that God's done in and through the two Ruths.

Bill—thank you for believing in my voice and for celebrating the significance of Christ-ward worship and praise.

Bob, Sherrie, and the wonderful people at Harvest House Publishers—thank you for championing my message and artistic vision once again.

RUTH CHOU SIMONS is a bestselling author, entrepreneur, and speaker. She shares her journey of God's grace intersecting daily life through word and paintbrush at GraceLaced.com, her popular blog, online shoppe, and Instagram community of more than a hundred thousand. Ruth and her husband, Troy, are grateful parents to six boys—their greatest adventure. Ruth's first book, *GraceLaced*, won a 2018 Christian Book Award.

Find Ruth—her art and heart—at gracelaced.com,
and at @gracelaced on Instagram, Facebook, and Twitter.

Other Books available from

RUTH CHOU SIMONS